Christmas
2009

Merry Christmas
Johanna!
Love,
Mom 'n Dad

500
cakes

500
cakes

the only cake compendium you'll ever need

Susannah Blake

SELLERS
PUBLISHING

A Quintet Book

Published by Sellers Publishing, Inc.
P.O. Box 818, Portland, Maine 04104
For ordering information:
(800) 625-3386 Toll Free
(207) 772-6814 Fax
Visit our Web site: www.sellerspublishing.com
E-mail: rsp@rsvp.com

ISBN: 978-1-4162-0534-0
Library of Congress Control Number: 2008933665
QTT.PCK

This book was conceived, designed, and produced by
Quintet Publishing Limited
6 Blundell Street
London N7 9BH
United Kingdom

Project Editor: Asha Savjani
Photographer: Ian Garlick
Food Stylist: Fergal Connolly
Designer: Chris Taylor
Art Editor: Michael Charles
Managing Editor: Donna Gregory
Publisher: James Tavendale

10 9 8 7 6 5 4 3 2 1

Printed in China by SNP Leefung Printers Ltd.

Shutterstock images appear on pages 15, 16, 20, 26
Stock Food images appear on pages 8, 11, 12, 19

contents

introduction

Nothing quite beats a home-baked cake. Cakes are wonderful for any occasion – whether it's an everyday cake for the kids when they get home from school, a luscious layered gateau to serve as dessert at a dinner party, a three-tiered wedding cake for your special day, or an old-fashioned favorite for afternoon tea. And then of course there are cheesecakes – more of a dessert with their creamy, melt-in-the-mouth filling, but a cake nevertheless.

Cakes are easy to make and incredibly versatile. Loaf cakes – cakes baked in a bread loaf pan – are very simple and often don't even need frosting. They're easy to slice and make a great choice for a family-friendly cake, and they're also terrific for wrapping up in foil and taking on a picnic. Layer cakes – cakes layered or sandwiched together with a filling – are a great way to transform simple classic sponge cakes into spectacular occasion cakes and decadent desserts, while big sheet cakes are the perfect choice when you need to feed a large number of people.

Cakes are obviously a must for birthdays and other celebrations, but there's no fixed rule about what type you have to serve. Just choose a recipe to suit the person you're baking for, think about what they like best, then find a cake recipe and decorations to match. A birthday cake is wonderful when it's aglow with candles, but there's no reason why you can't use sparklers instead or some other fabulously over-the-top decorations. There's also no reason why you can't celebrate a birthday with a simple plain cake dusted with cocoa powder.

Cakes make terrific gifts too – whether it's a dessert to take with you when you're invited to dinner or just a little something to make a friend feel special. There's very little better than opening your front door to someone holding a cake made just for you.

equipment

The majority of cakes can be made with fairly standard kitchen equipment. The only special items you'll need are baking pans themselves, and possibly some decorating equipment.

cake pans
Cake pans come in a great array of shapes and sizes. The main shapes are round, square, rectangular, and loaf, although you can also find more unusual shapes such as hearts, numbers, and letters. Pans may be loose-based or have a fixed base. Springform pans with a clip on the side also make unmolding easier. Although cake pans are most often made of metal, soft silicone baking pans are becoming more common. These don't get hot in the same way as metal does, so they are a good choice when you're baking with children.

measuring cups & spoons
Accurate measuring is absolutely essential for baking. If the proportions and quantities aren't quite right, your cake may not set or rise properly and you won't achieve the desired texture and flavor.

mixing bowls & spoons
A large mixing bowl and a wooden spoon are essentials for cake making. You may also find it useful to have a couple of smaller bowls for holding measured ingredients, or for mixing smaller quantities. A heatproof bowl is useful for melting ingredients such as chocolate and butter. A large metal spoon will be useful for folding ingredients such as whisked egg whites into cake mixtures.

other useful utensils

Rotary or electric whisks are great for whisking eggs and whipping cream, while spatulas are useful for scraping mixtures out of a bowl and for spreading on fillings and frostings. A metal skewer is very handy for inserting into a cake to check it has cooked properly all the way through.

wire rack

Unless otherwise stated, cakes should usually be transferred to a wire rack to cool to allow air to circulate underneath and prevent the cake from becoming soggy.

sieves or sifters

A large and small sieve (or sifter) will prove invaluable. The large size can be used for sifting ingredients such as flour and confectioners' sugar into a mixing bowl, while a small sieve can be used to dust finished cakes with confectioners' sugar or cocoa powder.

chopping boards & knives

These will be useful for all kinds of ingredient preparation, such as chopping chocolate, nuts, and large dried fruits. A large serrated knife will come in handy for slicing cakes horizontally before filling, and an unserrated knife is essential for slicing a fine-grained sponge cake or anything with bits in it.

waxed paper

Waxed paper is essential for lining cake pans to make unmolding easier.

timer

Accurate timing, like measuring, is essential in baking — so invest in a timer to avoid forgetting about your cake as it bakes. No one likes a burnt cake!

electric mixers

These devices are an absolute boon to the busy cook. They can take all the effort out of beating butter and sugar or other ingredients together — but remember that it's always best to fold the flour in yourself, rather than letting the machine do it for you.

ingredients

Most cakes are based on four basic ingredients — butter, sugar, eggs, and flour — and although there are a few cakes that defy this rule, they are few and far between. Once you have these basics, you can add other ingredients, such as chocolate, vanilla extract, lemon, nuts, and fruit, to add flavor and texture.

butter & other fats

Butter is usually the number one choice of fat for cakes, but margarine and oils may be used in some recipes instead. Unsalted butter is particularly good for making cakes because of its texture and flavor. If you suffer from a dairy intolerance or allergy, a nondairy margarine can be substituted for butter in most recipes. Generally, butter should be at room temperature and soft when you start baking.

sugar & sweeteners

You can use many different types of sugar to vary the taste and texture of cakes. White superfine sugar is most frequently used to sweeten cakes because it produces a cake with a deliciously fine texture. Coarser sugars will give a less good texture, although very coarse sugars such as demerara are good for sprinkling on top of cakes to produce a sweet, crunchy topping. Brown sugar adds color and a lovely rich flavor. (When measuring brown sugar by volume, make sure you pat it down firmly into the measuring cup.) Confectioners' sugar is mainly used for frostings and dusting and should be sifted before being combined with other ingredients. Some alternatives to sugar are honey, maple syrup, corn syrup, and molasses. Most often they are used in combination with sugar to give a distinct flavor and texture to the cake.

flour & leavening ingredients

Most cakes are made with self-rising wheat flour, or with all-purpose flour combined with a leavening ingredient, such as baking powder, baking soda, cream of tartar, or whisked egg whites. Where possible, recipes in this book are made with self-rising flour for ease of measuring. However, there are plenty of recipes using all-purpose flour as well. Other ingredients may also be used either in combination with, or instead of, wheat flour. These include ground almonds, potato flour, soy flour, rice flour, polenta, and buckwheat flour — all of which make a good choice if you are following a wheat- or gluten-free diet.

eggs

Adding eggs to a cake helps bind the ingredients together and enriches the cake. Eggs come in different sizes and it is important to use the egg size specified in a recipe; if no size is indicated, the use of a large egg is expected. Ideally, try to use the eggs at room temperature, and if you are whisking egg whites, be sure to use a very clean, grease-free bowl. If there is even a speck of grease, they will not whisk up properly.

other ingredients

Once you've got your basic cake batter, you can add all kinds of extra ingredients. Popular flavorings include vanilla extract, finely grated lemon and orange zest, coffee, unsweetened cocoa powder, and melted chocolate. Nuts, dried fruit, seeds, and chocolate chips add texture as well as flavor. Fresh fruit — berries, bananas, pineapple, cherries, apples, pears, apricots, and much, much more — make fantastic additions either in the batter or to decorate the top of a cake.

cake-making techniques

There are three basic types of cake mixture. Each one combines and uses the ingredients slightly differently to create a cake with its own unique taste and texture. These techniques may be adapted and tweaked from recipe to recipe, but as you bake the cakes in this book, you will find the same basic techniques used again and again.

classic sponge
One of the simplest cakes to make, a classic sponge cake, is usually made with equal quantities of butter, sugar, eggs, and flour, to which you can then add your own choice of flavoring such as vanilla, lemon, coffee, or chocolate. The recipe always begins with creaming together the butter and sugar until smooth. The eggs are then beaten in, and the flour sifted over the top and folded in. These types of cake can also be made with the all-in-one method – put all the ingredients together in a bowl and beat until creamy. If you use this method, make sure your butter is really soft before you start.

whisked sponge
A classic whisked sponge is made with eggs, sugar, flour, and very little fat, to create a very light sponge. The eggs and sugar are whisked together until thick and creamy, then the flour is sifted over the top, melted butter is added, and the whole mixture folded together. Because there is very little fat, these cakes do not store well and are best eaten on the day they are made. In some recipes, the initial cake batter is made with egg yolks only, then the whites are whisked and folded into the mixture. Cakes made using this technique usually use all-purpose flour because the whisked egg whites will leaven the cake on their own.

melted cake
In these cakes, ingredients such as butter, syrup or honey, and sugar are melted together in a pan, then left to cool before beating in the eggs and adding the flour. These cakes usually have a distinctive, moist, dense texture — popular examples include ginger cake, honey cake, and some fruit cakes.

greasing & lining cake pans
Before you make your cake, it's very important to prepare the cake pan. Most recipes call for it to be greased (use either butter or vegetable oil for this) and lined with waxed paper. The butter or oil for greasing has not been included in the list of ingredients for each recipe. I always line the bottom of the pan — it makes unmolding easier and neater. Just cut a piece of waxed paper to fit in the bottom of the pan. If the whole pan needs to be lined, cut a strip of waxed paper to fit around the sides as well. Many supermarkets and kitchen shops sell ready-made liners for loaf pans, which can make lining easier.

whisking, beating & folding
These are very common terms in baking. Whisking is done with a whisk — either light whisking to break up an egg, for example, or whisking until egg whites or whipping cream form soft/firm peaks. Beating is a vigorous mixing done with a wooden spoon or mixer, and with a fork in the case of "beating an egg." Beating is used for speed if, for example, you are breaking up an egg, or for efficiency if you're mixing together two substances such as sugar and butter. Folding is a gentler motion, using a large metal spoon. Slide the spoon down the side of the bowl, across the bottom, and through the mixture to combine the ingredients.

checking when a cake is "done"
Most cakes will look risen and be firm to the touch when they are cooked. A classic sponge will spring back when lightly pressed with your fingertips. One of the best methods for testing

this accurately is to insert a skewer into the center of the cake. If it is done, the skewer should come out clean. This technique won't work on all cakes though – for example, fudgy chocolate cakes may remain moist in the center – so always follow the advice given in the recipe. Because oven temperatures can vary from model to model, it's a good idea to check your cake for doneness a few minutes before the designated time. Some ovens have hot spots, so if you know this to be the case, turn your pan partway through cooking to ensure the cake bakes evenly.

decorating cakes

Adding the finishing, decorative touches to your cake is often the best part. There are so many wonderful variations to choose from and to combine — from filling and dusting to sprinkling, frosting, piping, and embellishing.

decorating unbaked cakes
An unbaked cake can be decorated by scattering nuts or fruit — for instance, whole or slivered almonds or blueberries — over the top so that when the cake bakes, the topping creates a decorative finish.

filling & sandwiching
Cakes can be transformed simply by splitting and filling them — or even more simply, by baking two thin cakes, then stacking them on top of each other with a filling in between. To split a cake, allow it to cool completely on a wire rack, then transfer it to a cutting board. Press down gently on the top of the cake with the flat of your hand, and use a long-bladed, unserrated thin knife to slice horizontally through the cake cleanly, in one go. You can use all kinds of fillings to sandwich the layers together. Jelly, whipped cream, fresh fruit, or buttercream are all excellent choices. Simply spread a generous layer over the bottom cake, then top with the second layer.

dusting
Probably the simplest of all decoration techniques is to add a pretty dusting of either confectioners' sugar or unsweetened cocoa powder to the top of the cake just before serving. Put a little sugar or cocoa in a small sieve, hold it over the top of the cake, and tap the edge to dust the cake lightly and evenly all over.

frosting

Topping your cake with a luscious, sugary frosting not only tastes great, but it will also add a very pretty finishing touch to your cake. There are all kinds of frosting — from the simplest glacé icing or buttercream to indulgent chocolate ganache and sophisticated royal icing. These can be drizzled, poured, swirled, spread, or piped — all giving different effects to your finished cake.

glacé icing

This very simple icing is particularly good for plain and fruity cakes. The basic icing is white, so try adding a few drops of food coloring to the finished icing to create pretty pastel shades. To make enough icing for an 8-in. (20-cm.) round cake, sift 1 1/2 cups of confectioners' sugar into a bowl, then stir in about 2 tablespoons boiling water or lemon juice until smooth and creamy. Pour or drizzle the icing over the cake.

buttercream

Another easy frosting, buttercream is great for topping and filling. For an 8-in. (20-cm.) round cake, beat together 6 tablespoons soft butter, a scant 1 1/4 cups confectioners' sugar, and 1 1/2 tablespoons milk until smooth and creamy. Swirl or spread the buttercream over your cake. You can use the frosting as it is or add flavorings such as 1/4 teaspoon vanilla extract, the finely grated zest of a lemon or orange, or 1 tablespoon unsweetened cocoa powder. Buttercream is suitable for tinting with food coloring.

cream cheese frosting

This all-American frosting is great on all kinds of cakes. It's a particular favorite for classic carrot cake. To frost an 8-in. (20-cm.) round cake, beat together 8 ounces of cream cheese, 1 1/3 cups confectioners' sugar, the finely grated zest of a lemon or lime, and 2 teaspoons lemon or lime juice. Leave plain or tint with food coloring, then spread or swirl over the cake.

chocolate ganache

Rich, dark, and with a wonderful, melt-in-the-mouth texture, chocolate ganache is probably the simplest — yet the most sophisticated — of all chocolate toppings. You can use ganache shortly after making if you want to pour it over the cake for a glossy finish, or you can let it cool and thicken if you want a spreading or swirling consistency. To frost an 8-in. (20-cm.) round cake, place 3 1/2 ounces of finely chopped semisweet chocolate in a heatproof bowl. Heat a generous 1/3 cup of whipping cream until almost boiling, then pour it over the chocolate to stand for 5 minutes. Stir until smooth, and then use immediately or wait to cool and thicken.

easy royal icing

This is the classic frosting used for fruity Christmas cakes and wedding cakes. It will harden to a crisp finish when left to dry for a couple of days. To cover the top and sides of an 8-in. (20-cm.) round cake, whisk 3 egg whites in a bowl until frothy, then whisk in 2 tablespoons lemon juice. Gradually whisk in about 1 1/2 pounds of confectioners' sugar until the mixture is thick and creamy and stands in peaks. Spread the icing over the cake to achieve a smooth effect, or swirl it up to give a ruffled, peaked effect. Although this frosting is most often used white, it may also be tinted with food coloring.

marzipan

If you're making a fruity Christmas cake, you will need to cover the cake in marzipan first, before frosting with royal icing. You can buy ready-made marzipan, but it's easy to make. Combine 2 1/2 cups ground almonds with 1/2 cup superfine sugar, then add 1 large beaten egg and 1 tablespoon lemon juice. Stir together well, tip out onto a clean work surface, knead until smooth, then wrap in plastic wrap until ready to use.

adding embellishments

Once your cake is frosted, you can add further embellishments if you want to create a real showstopper. If it's for a special occasion, you may want to tailor your decorations to the theme. For example, for a silver wedding anniversary, you could frost the cake with white frosting and sprinkle it with silver decorations and edible glitter. Or for Halloween, top your cake with creepy-crawly spiders.

sugared flower petals
Choose any edible flower petals you like, such as rose petals or violets. Brush the petals with egg white, dust with superfine sugar, and let dry before using to decorate. The finished flowers will glisten as if they have been dusted with frost.

chocolate curls
These elegant curls are wonderful for decorating chocolate cakes, cheesecakes, dessert cakes, and gateaux. Melt chocolate in a heatproof bowl set over a pan of barely simmering water. Pour the chocolate onto a marble slab or clean work surface and spread out in a thin layer, then leave to set. Using a sharp, flat-ended blade, such as a pastry scraper held at about 45 degrees, peel up layers of chocolate. As you scrape, the chocolate will curl into ruffled tubes.

chocolate shavings
These are even easier than making chocolate curls. Use a vegetable peeler to peel shavings of chocolate off a whole chocolate bar, or use a grater to make fine shavings.

silver dragées
These sweet little silver balls are wonderful on a frosted cake. Be warned, though, that they have recently become illegal in some states, so purchase yours from reputable retailers only.

foolproof cakes

There's a popular myth that baking is difficult, but that's nonsense! This chapter of easy-to-make and difficult-to-mess-up recipes proves the point. It's the ideal place to start, for anyone who's nervous about baking.

classic sheet cake

see variations page 50

Sheet cakes are perfect for birthdays or large celebrations when you need a cake to feed lots of people. A simple frosted cake covered with candles looks stunning.

for the cake
1 1/2 sticks butter, at room
    temperature
3/4 cup superfine sugar
3 eggs
scant 1 1/4 cups
    self-rising flour

1 tsp. baking powder
2 tbsp. milk
finely grated zest of 1 lemon
for the frosting
14 oz. (1 3/4 packages)
    cream cheese

1 1/3 cups confectioners'
    sugar, sifted
1 tbsp. lemon juice
yellow food coloring

Preheat the oven to 350°F (180°C). Grease an 8 x 12 or 9 x 13-in. (approximately 22 x 30-cm.) baking pan, then line the bottom with waxed paper.

Beat together the butter and sugar until pale and creamy, then beat in the eggs one at a time. Combine the flour and baking powder; sift the mixture over the top of the egg mixture; and fold in. Stir in the milk and lemon zest. Transfer the batter to the prepared pan and smooth the top. Bake for about 40 minutes or until risen and golden and a skewer inserted in the center comes out clean. Let the cake cool in the pan for about 10 minutes, then turn out onto a large wire rack to cool completely. To decorate, beat together the cream cheese, confectioners' sugar, and lemon juice until smooth and creamy, then add yellow food coloring to make a pretty pastel yellow. Swirl the frosting over the top and sides of the cake.

Serves 20

pound cake

see variations page 51

This is one of the all-time classic simple cakes that has been enjoyed for generations. Originally the cake was made with a pound each of butter, sugar, eggs, and flour — hence its name.

1 2/3 sticks butter, at room temperature
1 2/3 cups superfine sugar
6 eggs
2 1/2 cups self-rising flour

4 tbsp. milk
1 tsp. vanilla extract
confectioners' sugar, to dust

Preheat the oven to 350°F (180°C). Grease a 9-in. (22-cm.) round cake pan, then line the bottom with waxed paper.

Beat together the butter and sugar until pale and creamy, then beat in the eggs one at a time. Sift the flour over the mixture, then fold in. Stir in the milk and vanilla.

Spoon the cake batter into the prepared pan and smooth the top with the back of the spoon. Bake for about 1 hour or until risen and golden and a skewer inserted in the center comes out clean. Let it cool in the pan for a few minutes, then transfer to a wire rack to cool completely. Before serving, dust lightly with confectioners' sugar.

Serves 8

banana cake

see variations page 52

Soft, tender banana cake is an absolute classic and even better topped with an indulgent cream cheese frosting. It's also a great way to use up very ripe bananas that you think are a bit too soft to eat.

for the cake
2 ripe bananas
2 eggs
3/4 cup vegetable oil
3 tbsp. milk

1 1/2 cups light brown sugar
1 1/3 cups self-rising flour
1 tsp. ground cinnamon
1/2 tsp. ground ginger

for the frosting
7 oz. cream cheese
2/3 cup confectioners' sugar, sifted
1 tsp. lemon juice

Preheat oven to 350°F (180°C). Grease an 8-in. (20-cm.) round cake pan, then line the bottom with waxed paper.

Roughly mash the bananas in a large bowl, then beat in the eggs. Stir in the oil and milk. Break up any lumps in the brown sugar, then stir it into the banana mixture until well combined. Sift the flour and spices over the mixture, then fold in.

Tip the mixture into the prepared pan. Bake for 1 hour until a skewer inserted in the center comes out clean. Let cool in the pan for 10 minutes, then turn out onto a wire rack to cool completely.

To make the frosting, beat together the cream cheese, confectioners' sugar, and lemon juice until smooth and creamy, then spread over the cooled cake.

Serves 8

old-fashioned ginger cake

see variations page 53

Nothing quite beats a slice of rich, dark ginger cake. This one is even better a few days after baking; so if you can, make it a few days in advance, wrap tightly, and store in an airtight container until ready to serve.

3 1/3 cups all-purpose flour
1/2 tsp. salt
1 tbsp. baking powder
1 tsp. baking soda

2 tsp. ground ginger
3/4 cup dark molasses
3/4 cup light corn syrup
1 1/2 sticks butter, diced

generous 3/4 cup milk
3 pieces of stem ginger in
    syrup, roughly chopped

Preheat the oven to 350°F (180°C). Grease a 9-in. (22-cm.) round cake pan and line the bottom with waxed paper.

Combine the flour, salt, baking powder, baking soda, and ginger. Sift into a large bowl. Make a well in the middle.

Put the molasses, corn syrup, and butter in a pan and warm gently until the butter has melted and the mixture is smooth and combined. Stir in the milk and stem ginger. Pour the mixture into the well in the middle of the dry ingredients. Mix well to make a smooth batter.

Pour the batter into the prepared pan and bake for about 1 1/2 hours until risen and firm to the touch. Let cake cool in the pan for about 10 minutes, then transfer to a wire rack to cool completely.

Serves 8

boiled fruit cake

see variations page 54

This simple technique gives wonderfully moist results. The dried fruit plumps up in the tea before being baked in the cake, creating a cake packed with juicy, tangy fruit.

2 1/4 cups top-quality dried mixed fruit
1/2 cup demerara sugar
2/3 cup black tea
1 stick butter
1 1/2 cups self-rising flour

1/4 tsp. ground ginger
1/2 tsp. ground cinnamon
good pinch of ground nutmeg
2 eggs, lightly beaten

Put the fruit, sugar, tea, and butter in a saucepan. Bring to a boil. Reduce the heat and simmer for about 20 minutes, stirring frequently. Remove the pan from the heat and let it cool for about 20 minutes.

While the mixture cools, preheat the oven to 325°F (170°C). Grease an 8-in. (20-cm.) round cake pan and line its bottom with waxed paper. Sift the flour and spices into a large bowl, then add the cooled fruit mixture and eggs and quickly mix together. Spoon the mixture into the prepared cake pan, smoothing the top with the back of the spoon, and bake for 30 minutes. Reduce the temperature to 300°F (150°C) and bake for an additional 1 1/4 to 1 1/2 hours until a skewer inserted in the center comes out clean.

Let the cake cool in the pan for about 10 minutes, then transfer to a wire rack to cool completely.

Serves 8

simple chocolate sponge cake

see variations page 55

Everyone loves chocolate cake. With this can't-go-wrong recipe for chocolate sponge cake sandwiched with cherry jelly, you'll be everyone's favorite cook.

1 1/2 sticks butter, at room temperature
3/4 cup superfine sugar
3 eggs
scant 1 1/4 cups self-rising flour
3 tbsp. unsweetened cocoa powder

to decorate
4 tbsp. cherry jelly
unsweetened cocoa powder, to dust

Preheat the oven to 350°F (180°C). Grease two 8-in. (20-cm.) round cake pans and line the bottoms with waxed paper.

Beat together the butter and sugar until pale and fluffy. Beat in the eggs one at a time. Sift the flour and cocoa over the top, then fold in.

Spoon the cake batter into the prepared pans and spread out evenly using the back of the spoon. Bake for 20 to 25 minutes until golden brown and a skewer inserted in the center comes out clean. Turn the cakes out onto a wire rack and let cool completely.

To serve, spread the cherry jelly over one of the cakes. Top with the second cake. Dust with cocoa powder.

Serves 8

date & walnut loaf

see variations page 56

This version of the classic date and nut bread is simple and flavorful without being too sweet. It contains less butter than many loaf cakes, making it a great option if you're looking for a treat without too much guilt.

scant 1 cup pitted dates, chopped
1 tbsp. clear honey, plus extra for brushing
generous 3/4 cup boiling water
1 stick butter, at room temperature

1/2 cup light brown sugar
1 egg
2/3 cup walnut pieces
2 cups self-rising flour

Put the dates in a bowl with the honey, cover with the boiling water, and let soak for about 1 hour until cool. Preheat the oven to 350°F (180°C). Grease an 8 1/2 x 4 1/2-in. (2 lb.) loaf pan, and line the bottom with waxed paper.

Beat together the butter and sugar until smooth and creamy, then beat in the egg. Gradually beat in the dates and soaking liquid (don't worry if the mixture curdles) and stir in about three-quarters of the nuts. Sift the flour over the mixture, one-third at a time, then fold in.

Spoon into the prepared pan, smooth the top with the back of the spoon, and sprinkle the remaining nuts on top.

Bake for about 1 hour until a skewer inserted in the center comes out clean. Let cool in the pan for 10 minutes, then turn out on a wire rack, brush the top with honey, and let cool completely.

Serves 8

lemon drizzle cake

see variations page 57

This cake is an absolute classic and utterly simple to make. The intense lemony flavor comes from drenching the tender golden cake with lemon syrup while it's still warm.

for the cake
1 stick plus 1 tbsp. butter, at room temperature
2/3 cup superfine sugar
2 extra-large eggs
finely grated zest of 1 lemon

1 cup self-rising flour
for the topping
6 tbsp. superfine sugar
juice of 1 lemon

Preheat the oven to 350°F (180°C). Line an 8-in. (20-cm.) springform square cake pan with waxed paper.

Beat together the butter and sugar until pale and creamy. Beat in the eggs, one at a time, then stir in the lemon zest. Sift the flour over the mixture, then fold in. Tip the mixture into the lined pan and smooth out evenly. Bake for about 20 minutes until risen and golden, and a skewer inserted in the center comes out clean.

Place the cake pan on a cooling rack. Prick the top of the cake all over with a skewer.

Combine the sugar and lemon juice and immediately pour over the top of the cake. Let the cake cool in the pan, then carefully unmold. Cut into squares and serve.

Serves 9–12

vanilla layer cake

see variations page 58

Everyone loves a layer cake, and this recipe is the easiest one in the world to make. Just make sure the cakes are completely cool before you spread them with the buttercream frosting.

for the cake
1 1/2 sticks butter, at room temperature
3/4 cup superfine sugar
3 eggs
scant 1 1/4 cups self-rising flour
1 tsp. vanilla extract

for the frosting
scant 2 cups confectioners' sugar, sifted
1 stick butter, at room temperature
1/4 tsp. vanilla extract
2 tbsp. milk

Preheat the oven to 350°F (180°C). Grease two 8-in. (20-cm.) round cake pans, and line the bottoms with waxed paper.

Beat together the butter and sugar until pale and fluffy. Beat in the eggs one at a time. Sift the flour on top and fold in, then stir in the vanilla. Spoon the cake batter into the prepared pans and spread out evenly, using the back of the spoon. Bake for 20 to 25 minutes until golden brown and a skewer inserted in the center comes out clean. Turn the cakes out onto a wire rack and let cool completely.

To make the frosting, beat together the confectioners' sugar, butter, vanilla, and milk until smooth and creamy. Spread slightly less than half the frosting over one cake and place the second cake on top. Swirl on the remaining frosting.

Serves 8

cherry & marzipan loaf cake

see variations page 59

Layering the cake with marzipan gives this golden cake a lusciously sticky and indulgent center. It's particularly good served warm for afternoon tea or morning coffee.

1 1/2 sticks butter, at room temperature
3/4 cup superfine sugar
3 eggs
scant 1 1/4 cups self-rising flour

scant 1 cup ground almonds
3/4 cup candied cherries, quartered
4 oz. marzipan, finely grated
confectioners' sugar, for dusting

Preheat the oven to 350°F (180°C). Grease an 8 1/2 x 4 1/2-in. (2 lb.) loaf pan, and line the bottom with waxed paper.

Beat together the butter and sugar until pale and creamy, then beat in the eggs one at a time. Sift the flour and ground almonds over the mixture, then fold in. Scatter the cherries over the mixture, then fold in until evenly distributed.

Spoon half the batter into the loaf pan and smooth out evenly. Sprinkle the marzipan on top. Cover with the remaining batter and smooth out evenly. Bake for about 45 minutes. Cover the top of the cake with foil, then bake for an additional 25 minutes until risen and golden and a skewer inserted in the center comes out clean.

Let the cake cool in the pan for about 10 minutes, then lift out onto a wire rack to cool. Serve slightly warm from the oven or at room temperature, dusted with confectioners' sugar.

Serves 8

orange refrigerator cake

see variations page 60

The perfect recipe for anyone afraid of baking—because there's no baking involved! Just assemble the ingredients, then chill overnight before turning out a luscious, creamy cake.

1/3 cup toasted hazelnuts, roughly chopped
8 oz. mascarpone cheese
2 tbsp. confectioners' sugar, sifted
finely grated zest of 1 orange

juice of 2 oranges
one 3-oz. package soft ladyfingers
2 whole oranges

Line an 8 1/2 x 4 1/2-in. (2 lb.) loaf pan with a large piece of plastic wrap, allowing it to hang down over the edges. Scatter the hazelnuts over the bottom in an even layer.

Beat the mascarpone until soft, then beat in the confectioners' sugar and orange zest. Beat in the orange juice a little at a time until the mixture is smooth and creamy. Spoon slightly more than one-third of the mixture over the nuts, then top with a layer of ladyfingers. Cut the zest and white pith off the oranges, then slice between the membranes to remove the wedges of flesh, reserving any juice. Arrange the orange flesh on top of the ladyfingers.

Spoon the remaining mascarpone mixture on top, then top with another layer of ladyfingers and drizzle with any reserved juice. Gently pull the plastic wrap over the top and press down very gently all over the top with the tips of your fingers.

Chill for about 4 hours. Place a plate over the pan and flip over, then return to the fridge for 4 more hours or overnight.

To serve, turn the cake back into the pan and unfold the plastic wrap. Turn the cake out onto a serving plate and gently peel away the plastic wrap.

Serves 8

easy lime loaf cake

see variations page 61

Fresh, zesty, and oh-so-simple, this delicious golden cake is fabulous served with a cup of afternoon tea. It's also the perfect treat to go in a lunchbox or picnic basket.

for the cake
1 1/2 sticks butter, at room temperature
3/4 cup superfine sugar
3 eggs
scant 1 1/4 cups self-rising flour

finely grated zest and juice of 2 limes
for the syrup
finely grated zest and juice of 2 limes
generous 1/3 cup superfine sugar

Preheat the oven to 350°F (180°C). Grease an 8 1/2 x 4 1/2-in. (2 lb.) loaf pan, then line the bottom with waxed paper.

Beat together the butter and sugar until pale and creamy. Beat in the eggs one at a time. Sift the flour over the top and fold in, then stir in the lime zest and juice. Spoon the mixture into the prepared pan and spread out evenly, using the back of the spoon. Bake for about 50 minutes until golden brown and a skewer inserted in the center comes out clean. Let the cake cool in the pan for about 5 minutes, then transfer to a wire rack to cool completely.

Meanwhile, make the syrup. Put the lime zest and juice in a pan with the sugar, then heat gently, stirring until the sugar has dissolved completely. Bring to a boil and cook for 1 minute. Remove from the heat and cool slightly until the syrup starts to thicken. Pour over the warm cake and let stand for at least 30 minutes before serving.

Serves 8

variations

classic sheet cake

see base recipe page 29

chocolate sheet cake
Prepare the basic recipe, adding 3 tablespoons unsweetened cocoa with the flour, and omitting the lemon zest. To make the frosting, add 2 tablespoons unsweetened cocoa and use milk instead of lemon juice.

vanilla sheet cake
Prepare the basic recipe, using 1 1/2 teaspoons vanilla extract instead of the lemon zest. To make the frosting, use milk instead of the lemon juice and add 1 teaspoon vanilla extract.

candy sheet cake
Prepare the basic recipe, using lilac food coloring in place of yellow. Decorate the top of the cake with brightly colored candies such as M&Ms or sprinkles.

coffee sheet cake
Prepare the basic recipe, replacing the lemon zest with 1 tablespoon instant coffee dissolved in 1 tablespoon boiling water. For the frosting, replace the lemon juice with 1 tablespoon instant coffee dissolved in 1 tablespoon boiling water. Decorate the top of the cake with walnut halves or toasted hazelnuts.

variations

pound cake

see base recipe page 31

lemon pound cake
Prepare the basic recipe, substituting the finely grated zest of 1 lemon for the vanilla extract.

orange pound cake
Prepare the basic recipe, substituting the finely grated zest of 1 orange for the vanilla extract. Once the cake is cooled, prick all over using a skewer and brush over some orange juice sweetened with superfine sugar.

cherry pound cake
Prepare the basic recipe, adding 2/3 cup chopped glacé cherries to the cake mixture. Frost with icing.

walnut pound cake
Prepare the basic recipe, adding 1/2 cup roughly chopped walnuts to the cake mixture.

chocolate pound cake
Prepare the basic recipe, adding 4 tablespoons unsweetened cocoa powder with the flour. Spread the top of the cooled cake with melted chocolate, and once set, dust with cocoa powder.

variations

banana cake

see base recipe page 32

banana ginger cake
Prepare the basic recipe, stirring 2 chopped pieces of stem ginger in syrup into the mixture with the milk.

simple banana cake
Prepare the basic recipe, omitting the frosting.

banana walnut cake
Prepare the basic recipe, adding 2/3 cup walnut pieces after stirring in the sugar.

banana pecan cake
Prepare the basic recipe, adding 2/3 cup roughly chopped pecans after stirring in the sugar.

banana chocolate cake
Prepare the basic recipe, adding 3/4 cup chopped bittersweet chocolate after stirring in the sugar, and topping with melted chocolate rather than frosting. Decorate with sliced banana.

variations

old-fashioned ginger cake

see base recipe page 35

golden ginger cake
Prepare the basic recipe, omitting the molasses and using an additional
3/4 cup corn syrup.

ginger orange cake
Prepare the basic recipe, adding the finely grated zest of 1 orange with the
stem ginger.

ginger lemon cake
Prepare the basic recipe, adding the finely grated zest of 1 lemon with the
stem ginger.

ginger lime cake
Prepare the basic recipe, adding the finely grated zest of 2 limes with the
stem ginger.

chocolate ginger cake
Prepare the basic recipe, adding 3/4 cup chopped bittersweet chocolate with
the stem ginger.

variations

boiled fruit cake

see base recipe page 36

boiled fruit cake with walnuts
Prepare the basic recipe, adding 1/3 cup roughly chopped walnuts to the flour with the dried fruit mixture and eggs.

boiled fruit cake with almonds
Prepare the basic recipe, adding 3 tablespoons slivered almonds to the flour with the dried fruit mixture and eggs.

boiled apricot fruit cake
Prepare the basic recipe, using 1 1/3 cups mixed dried fruit and 1 cup roughly chopped dried apricots instead of the 2 1/4 cups mixed fruit.

boiled figgy fruit cake
Prepare the basic recipe, using 1 1/3 cups mixed dried fruit and 1 cup roughly chopped dried figs instead of the 2 1/4 cups mixed fruit.

boiled prune fruit cake
Prepare the basic recipe, using 1 1/3 cups mixed dried fruit and 1 cup roughly chopped dried prunes instead of the 2 1/4 cups mixed fruit.

simple chocolate sponge cake

see base recipe page 37

chocolate–hazelnut sponge cake
Prepare the basic recipe, folding 1/2 cup roughly chopped hazelnuts into the cake batter before baking. Substitute chocolate hazelnut spread for the cherry jelly.

chocolate–cream sponge cake
Prepare the basic recipe, spreading about 1/2 cup whipped cream over the jelly before topping with the second cake layer.

chocolate–orange sponge cake
Prepare the basic recipe, folding the finely grated zest of 1 orange into the cake batter before baking. Substitute orange curd for the cherry jelly.

simple mocha sponge cake
Prepare the basic recipe, folding 2 teaspoons instant coffee dissolved in 1 tablespoon boiling water into the cake batter before baking. Substitute 1/2 cup whipped cream for the cherry jelly.

double chocolate chip sponge cake
Prepare the basic recipe, folding 1/2 cup semisweet chocolate chips into the cake batter before baking.

variations

date & walnut loaf

see base recipe page 39

spiced date & walnut loaf
Prepare the basic recipe, adding 1 teaspoon apple pie spice with the flour.

ginger, date & walnut loaf
Prepare the basic recipe, adding 3 roughly chopped pieces of stem ginger in syrup with the egg and 1 teaspoon ground ginger with the flour.

fig & walnut loaf
Prepare the basic recipe, substituting chopped dried figs for the dates.

date & pecan loaf
Prepare the basic recipe, substituting roughly chopped pecans for the walnuts.

date & brazil nut loaf
Prepare the basic recipe, substituting roughly chopped Brazil nuts in place of the walnuts.

lemon drizzle cake

see base recipe page 40

lime drizzle cake
Prepare the basic recipe, using the finely grated zest of 2 limes instead of the lemon zest and the juice of 2 limes instead of the lemon juice.

passionfruit and lemon drizzle cake
Prepare the basic recipe, omitting the topping. Instead, press the pulp from 6 passionfruit through a sieve, then stir in 2 tbsp superfine sugar and drizzle over the cake.

lemon drizzle dessert cake
Prepare the basic recipe. Instead of cutting it in squares, cut it in rectangular fingers, arrange each one on an elegant dessert plate, and top with a generous spoonful of crème fraîche.

fruity lemon drizzle cake
Prepare the basic recipe, folding a generous 1/2 cup of mixed dried cherries and blueberries into the cake batter, before transferring to the pan.

variations

vanilla layer cake

see base recipe page 43

chocolate layer cake
Prepare the basic recipe, replacing the vanilla in the cake batter with
2 tablespoons unsweetened cocoa powder, sifted in with the flour. Replace
the vanilla in the frosting with 1 1/2 tablespoons unsweetened cocoa powder.

lemon layer cake
Replace the vanilla in the cake batter with the finely grated zest of 1 lemon.
For the frosting, substitute the finely grated zest of 1/2 lemon for the vanilla
and use lemon juice instead of milk.

almond layer cake
Replace the vanilla in the batter with 1/3 cup ground almonds. Replace the
vanilla in the frosting with almond essence. Decorate with slivered almonds.

strawberry layer cake
Spread 4 tablespoons strawberry jelly on the bottom cake layer, before
topping with the buttercream and the second layer.

black currant layer cake
Spread 4 tablespoons black currant jelly on the bottom cake, top with
buttercream and add the second layer.

cherry & marzipan loaf cake

see base recipe page 44

apple loaf cake
Prepare the basic recipe, adding 1 3/4 cups chopped, peeled apple and
the finely grated zest of 1 lemon to the batter, instead of the cherries and
almonds. Omit the marzipan.

cherry & lemon loaf cake
Prepare the basic recipe, adding the finely grated zest of 1 lemon with the
cherries. Omit the marzipan.

cherry & almond loaf cake
Prepare the basic recipe, omitting the marzipan.

chocolate & marzipan loaf cake
Prepare the basic recipe, substituting 3/4 cup chopped bittersweet chocolate
for the cherries.

prune & marzipan loaf cake
Prepare the basic recipe, substituting 1 1/4 cups roughly chopped prunes for
the cherries.

variations

orange refrigerator cake

see base recipe page 46

orange–pistachio refrigerator cake
Prepare the basic recipe, using roughly chopped pistachio nuts to replace the hazelnuts.

orange–almond refrigerator cake
Prepare the basic recipe, using roughly chopped almonds instead of the hazelnuts.

peach refrigerator cake
Prepare the basic recipe, replacing the orange flesh with 2 peeled peaches, cut into wedges.

strawberry refrigerator cake
Prepare the basic recipe, replacing the orange flesh with about 2 cups sliced fresh strawberries.

raspberry refrigerator cake
Prepare the basic recipe, replacing the orange flesh with about 2 cups gently crushed raspberries.

easy lime loaf cake

see base recipe page 49

lime & coconut loaf
Prepare the basic recipe, folding 1 scant cup shredded coconut into the cake with the flour.

lime & pistachio loaf
Prepare the basic recipe, folding 1/2 cup roughly chopped pistachio nuts into the cake with the lime zest and juice. Add 1/3 cup roughly chopped pistachios to the syrup before pouring it over the cake.

lime & blueberry loaf
Prepare the basic recipe, folding 2/3 cup dried blueberries into the batter.

lime & cranberry loaf
Prepare the basic recipe, folding 2/3 cup dried cranberries into the cake with the lime zest and juice.

frosted lime loaf
Prepare the basic recipe, replacing the lime syrup with a lime drizzle frosting. To make the frosting, stir together the finely grated zest and juice of 1 lime with 3/4 cup sifted confectioners' sugar until smooth and creamy. Pour over the cooled cake.

classic cakes

When you think of cake, it's often the classics that spring to mind. This chapter helps you rediscover your old favorites and beloved childhood treats, or choose a contemporary classic.

madeira cake

see variations page 88

Sometimes the simplest cakes are the best, and this plain, golden, lemony loaf is no exception. It was traditionally served with a glass of Madeira wine in the nineteenth century (hence its name). It's just as delicious with a cup of tea or coffee.

2 sticks butter, at room temperature
generous 3/4 cup superfine sugar, plus 1-2 tbsp.
   for sprinkling
3 extra-large eggs

1 1/2 cups self-rising flour
1/3 cup all-purpose flour
finely grated zest and juice of 1 lemon

Preheat the oven to 325°F (160°C). Grease an 8 1/2 x 4 1/2-in. (2 lb.) loaf pan, and line the bottom with waxed paper.

Beat together the butter and sugar until pale and creamy, then beat in the eggs one at a time. Sift the flour over the mixture, then fold it in. Fold in the lemon zest and juice.

Spoon the batter into the prepared pan, smoothing the top with the back of the spoon. Sprinkle the top with 1-2 tbsp. sugar and bake for about 55 minutes, or until a skewer inserted in the center comes out clean.

Let the cake cool in the pan for about 10 minutes before turning it out onto a wire rack to cool completely.

Serves 8

carrot cake

see variations page 87

There are a great many variations of this classic cake, but this one flavored with orange, cinnamon, and ginger is particularly good. The combination of sweet, crumbly sponge cake and rich, creamy frosting is hard to beat.

for the cake
3/4 cup light brown sugar
1/4 cup superfine sugar
1 cup vegetable oil
3 eggs
finely grated zest of 1 orange

1 tsp. ground cinnamon
1/2 tsp. ground ginger
2 cups self-rising flour
2 large carrots, grated (about
    2 cups)
3/4 cup chopped walnuts

for the frosting
7 oz. cream cheese
1 tsp. lemon juice
2/3 cup confectioners' sugar,
    sifted

Preheat the oven to 350°F (180°C). Grease an 8-in. (20-cm.) round cake pan and line the bottom with waxed paper.

Beat together the sugars, oil, and eggs. Stir in the orange zest, cinnamon, and ginger. Sift the flour over the bowl, then fold in. Fold in the carrots and walnuts. Tip the mixture into the prepared cake pan and spread out evenly. Bake for 1 to 1 1/4 hours or until a skewer inserted in the center comes out clean. Turn out onto a wire rack to cool completely.

To make the frosting, beat together the cream cheese, lemon juice, and sugar. Spread it over the cooled cake. To serve, cut into wedges.

Serves 8

victoria sandwich

see variations page 89

This is an all-time classic British cake named for Queen Victoria. Traditionally, it is split and filled with jelly, then dusted simply with confectioners' sugar. This version is made of two layers of sponge cake sandwiched with fresh raspberries, jelly, and cream.

1 1/2 sticks butter, at room
   temperature
3/4 cup superfine sugar
3 eggs

scant 1 1/4 cups self-rising
   flour

to decorate
3 1/2 tbsp. raspberry jelly

1 1/4 cups fresh raspberries
1/2 cup whipping cream
confectioners' sugar, for dusting

Preheat the oven to 350°F (180°C). Grease two 8-in. (20-cm.) springform round cake pans, and line the bottoms with waxed paper. Beat together the butter and sugar until pale and fluffy. Beat in the eggs one at a time. Sift the flour over the egg mixture, then stir it in until thoroughly combined.

Spoon the cake batter into the prepared pans and spread out evenly, using the back of the spoon. Bake for 20 to 25 minutes until golden brown and the cake springs back when pressed lightly with the tips of your fingers. Turn the cakes out onto a wire rack, gently peel off the waxed paper, and let cool completely.

Just before serving, spread the jelly over the top of one cake layer and top with the raspberries. Whip the cream until it stands in soft peaks, then spread it on top of the berries.

Top with the second cake layer and dust with confectioners' sugar. Serve immediately.

Serves 8

dundee cake

see variations page 90

This citrusy version of the English fruit cake improves with keeping, so if you can, make it a week in advance and store in an airtight container until ready to serve.

1 1/2 sticks butter
1/2 cup superfine sugar
generous 1/4 cup light brown sugar
3 eggs
finely grated zest of 1 orange
1 1/3 cups self-rising flour

1 tsp. baking powder
2 tbsp. brandy
1 1/3 cups mixed dried vine fruits (raisins,
    golden raisins, currants)
1/4 cup candied cherries, halved
1/3 cup blanched almonds

Preheat the oven to 325°F (160°C). Line the base and sides of a 7-in. (18-cm.) round cake pan with waxed paper.

Cream the butter and sugars together until fluffy, then beat in the eggs one at a time. Stir in the orange zest, then sift the flour and baking powder over the top and stir in. Mix in the brandy followed by the dried vine fruits and candied cherries.

Tip the mixture into the prepared pan, spreading it out evenly, then arrange the almonds on top in concentric circles. Bake for about 1 hour 10 minutes until dark golden and a skewer inserted in the center comes out clean.

Let cool in the pan for about 20 minutes, then turn out onto a wire rack to cool completely. Wrap in aluminum foil, and store in an airtight container until ready to serve.

Serves 8

coffee & walnut cake

see variations page 91

Coffee and walnuts are a sublime pairing in this golden, crumbly cake with its rich coffee butter frosting. A favorite for generations and an absolute must on any tea table.

for the cake
1 1/2 sticks butter, at room temperature
generous 3/4 cup superfine sugar
3 eggs
1 1/4 cups self-rising flour

1/2 cup walnut pieces
2 1/2 tsp. instant coffee, dissolved in 1 tbsp. hot water
for the frosting
2 tbsp. milk
2 tsp. instant coffee

3/4 stick butter, at room temperature
1 1/4 cups confectioners' sugar, sifted
walnut halves, to decorate

Preheat the oven to 350°F (180°C). Grease two 8-in. (20-cm.) round cake pans, and line the bottoms with waxed paper. Beat the butter and sugar together until pale and creamy, then beat in the eggs one at a time. Sift the flour over the butter mixture and stir in. Fold in the walnuts and coffee. Divide the mixture between the cake pans and spread out evenly. Bake for 20 to 25 minutes until golden and the cake springs back when pressed gently. Transfer to a wire rack to cool.

To make the frosting, warm the milk and coffee in a pan, stirring until the coffee has dissolved. Pour into a bowl, leaving to cool until just warm before adding the butter and confectioners' sugar. Beat together until smooth and creamy. Spread slightly less than half of the frosting over one of the cooled cakes, then place the second cake on top. Spread the remaining frosting on top and decorate with walnut halves.

Serves 8

pineapple upside-down cake

see variations page 92

Everyone loves this retro classic, with its delicious flavor and melting golden texture.

3 tbsp. light brown sugar
4 canned pineapple rings
2 candied cherries, halved
1 stick butter, at room temperature
1/2 cup superfine sugar

finely grated zest of 1 lemon
2 eggs
3/4 cup self-rising flour
1/2 tsp. baking powder
2 tbsp. pineapple juice

Preheat the oven to 350°F (180°C). Generously grease an 8-in. (20-cm.) round cake pan, then sprinkle the brown sugar over the base and arrange the pineapple rings on top. Put a cherry half in the center of each pineapple ring and set aside.

Beat together the butter and superfine sugar until smooth and creamy. Beat in the lemon zest and the eggs, one at a time. Sift the flour and baking powder over the top and fold in. Stir in the pineapple juice.

Spoon the batter on top of the pineapple rings and smooth out using the back of the spoon. Bake for 25 to 30 minutes until a skewer inserted in the center comes out clean. Let the cake cool in the pan for about 15 minutes, then turn it out onto a serving plate. Serve warm or cold.

Serves 8

raspberry genoese

see variations page 93

This is the classic whisked sponge cake, and although the method sounds tricky, it's actually very simple. To enjoy it at its best, serve it on the day you make it.

3 eggs
1/3 cup superfine sugar
scant 1/2 cup self-rising flour, sifted

3 tbsp. melted butter
1 1/3 cups whipping cream
generous 3 cups fresh raspberries

Preheat the oven to 350°F (180°C). Grease two 7-in. (18-cm.) round cake pans, and line the bottoms with waxed paper.

Put the eggs and sugar in a heatproof bowl over a pan of barely simmering water, making sure the bowl does not touch the water. Whisk for about 10 minutes until the mixture is thick and pale and leaves a trail when the whisk is lifted out of the bowl.

Sift about three-quarters of the flour over the mixture and fold in. Sift the remaining flour over the mixture and gradually drizzle in the butter as you fold the mixture together. Spoon the batter into the prepared pans and bake for about 30 minutes until risen and golden, and a skewer inserted in the center comes out clean. Turn the cakes out onto a wire rack to cool completely.

Just before serving, whip the cream and spread slightly less than half over one cake layer. Sprinkle slightly less than half the raspberries over the whipped cream, then place the second cake layer on top. Top with the remaining whipped cream and raspberries, and serve.

Serves 8

marble cake

see variations page 94

This simple two-tone cake is always a favorite with children who love the marbled effect when the cake is sliced. This version, topped with creamy frosting and chocolate chips, makes it even more appealing.

for the cake
1 1/2 sticks butter, at room temperature
3/4 cup superfine sugar
3 eggs
scant 1 1/4 cups self-rising flour
1 tsp. vanilla extract
2 tbsp. unsweetened cocoa powder

for the frosting
3/4 stick butter, at room temperature
1 1/4 cups confectioners' sugar, sifted
1 tbsp. unsweetened cocoa powder, sifted
1–2 tbsp. milk
2 tbsp. semisweet chocolate chips, to decorate
2 tbsp. white chocolate chips, to decorate

Preheat the oven to 350°F (180°C). Grease an 8-in. (20-cm.) round cake pan, and line the bottom with waxed paper. Beat together the butter and sugar until pale and creamy, then beat in the eggs one at a time. Sift the flour over the top, then fold in. Divide the mixture between two bowls. Stir the vanilla extract into one; sift the cocoa over the other bowl and fold in. Place alternating spoonfuls of the two batters in the cake pan so you finish with distinctive dollops of brown and white batter. Drag a skewer through the dollops three or four times to give a marbled effect. Bake for about 45 minutes until risen and golden. Transfer to a wire rack and let it cool completely.

For the frosting, beat together the butter, sugar, cocoa, and 1 tbsp. of the milk until smooth. If necessary, add a little more milk, then spread over the cake. Sprinkle with chocolate chips.

Serves 8

orange poppyseed cake

see variations page 95

This classic cake is light and citrusy—great served with tea or coffee.

for the cake
1 1/2 sticks butter, at room temperature
3/4 cup superfine sugar
finely grated zest of 1 1/2 oranges
3 eggs
scant 1/4 cup self-rising flour

2 1/2 tbsp. poppyseeds
for the frosting
2 oranges
9 oz. mascarpone cheese
generous 1/2 cup confectioners' sugar, sifted

Preheat the oven to 350°F (180°C). Grease a 9-in. (23-cm.) round cake pan and line the bottom with waxed paper.

Beat the butter, sugar, and orange zest until pale and creamy, then beat in the eggs one at a time. Sift the flour over the mixture, then fold in. Fold in the poppyseeds. Spoon the mixture into the prepared pan, smooth the top, and bake for about 50 minutes until risen and golden and a skewer inserted in the center comes out clean. Let the cake cool in the pan for about 5 minutes, then turn out to cool on a wire rack.

To make the frosting, grate the zest from the oranges and set aside. Remove the rest of the zest and white pith from the oranges and slice between the membranes to neatly remove the segments of flesh. Set the segments aside. Beat the mascarpone, confectioners' sugar, and reserved zest until smooth and creamy. Swirl the frosting over the cake and decorate with the orange segments just before serving.

Serves 8–10

devil's food cake

see variations page 96

The antithesis of an angel food cake with its dark layers of chocolate sponge cake and creamy frosting, this cake is another classic that shouldn't be missed.

for the cake
1 1/2 sticks butter
1 1/3 cups superfine sugar
3/4 cup unsweetened cocoa powder
1 1/4 cups milk
3 eggs
2 cups all-purpose flour

1 1/2 tsp. baking powder
1/2 tsp. salt
for the frosting
7 oz. dark chocolate, finely chopped
1/4 stick butter, diced
generous 3/4 cup whipping cream

Preheat the oven to 350°F (180°C). Grease two 9-in. (23-cm.) round cake pans and line the bottoms with waxed paper.

Beat the butter and sugar together until pale and creamy. In a separate bowl, mix the cocoa with a little of the milk to make a smooth paste, then beat it into the butter and sugar mixture. Beat in the eggs one at a time. Combine the flour, baking powder, and salt. Sift about half into the chocolate mixture and fold in. Stir in the remaining milk, then sift in the remaining flour mixture and fold together. Divide the batter between the prepared pans and bake for about 25 minutes until risen, and a skewer inserted in the center comes out clean.

Let cool in the pans for about 5 minutes, then turn out onto a wire rack to cool completely. To make the frosting, put the chocolate and butter in a heatproof bowl. Heat the cream until

almost boiling, then pour it over the chocolate and butter and let stand for 5 minutes. Stir until smooth, then let cool until thick enough to spread. Spread slightly less than half over one cake, top with the second cake, and swirl the remaining frosting on top.

Serves 8–10

dark chocolate-mocha mud cake

see variations page 97

Rich and indulgent, this dark chocolate cake with its even darker frosting is the ultimate cake for hardened chocoholics!

for the cake
5 oz. bittersweet chocolate, chopped
2 sticks butter, diced
scant 2 cups superfine sugar
1 cup milk
2 tbsp. instant coffee

2 eggs
1 1/2 cups all-purpose flour
generous 1/3 cup self-rising flour
2 tbsp. unsweetened cocoa powder

for the frosting
3 1/2 oz. bittersweet chocolate, finely chopped
generous 1/3 cup whipping cream

Preheat the oven to 325°F (170°C). Grease an 8-in. (20-cm.) round cake pan and line the bottom with waxed paper. Put the chocolate, butter, sugar, milk, and coffee together in a large pan. Heat very gently, stirring, until the butter and chocolate have melted and the mixture is smooth. Remove from the heat and let cool for 15 minutes.

Beat in the eggs, then sift the flours and cocoa over the top and fold in. Tip the mixture into the prepared pan and bake for about 1 1/2 hours. Let cool in the pan for about 30 minutes, then turn out onto a wire rack to cool completely.

To make the frosting, put the chocolate in a heatproof bowl. Heat the cream until almost boiling, then pour it over the chocolate and let stand for 5 minutes. Stir until smooth, then let it cool and thicken slightly before pouring it over the cake.

Serves 8

raspberry swiss roll

see variations page 98

Also known as a jelly roll, this log-shaped cake with a spiral of jelly in its center is a real family favorite. This version includes fresh raspberries for an extra fruity, juicy treat. It is best served on the day it is made.

3 eggs
3/4 cup superfine sugar, plus extra for sprinkling
1/2 cup self-rising flour
1 tbsp. ground almonds

confectioners' sugar, to dust
4 tbsp. raspberry jelly
1 1/3 cups fresh raspberries, plus extra to serve

Preheat the oven to 220°F (425°C). Grease a 9 x 13-in. (22 x 32-cm.) jelly roll pan and line the bottom. Whisk the eggs and sugar for about 10 minutes until the mixture is thick and pale and leaves a trail when the whisk is lifted. Sift the flour over the egg mixture, add the almonds, and fold together. Turn the mixture into the prepared pan, easing it into the corners. Bake for about 10 minutes until golden and starting to shrink from the edges of the pan. Remove from oven. Meanwhile, lay a piece of waxed paper (slightly larger than the pan) on the work surface and sprinkle thickly with confectioners' sugar.

Turn out the cooked cake onto the sugar-dusted paper, peel off the lining paper, and snip off the cake corners to make it easier to roll. Spread jelly over the top of the hot cake, sprinkle the raspberries on top, then roll up tightly using the waxed paper. Let stand for about 5 minutes. Transfer the roll to a wire rack to cool completely. Serve dusted with confectioners' sugar and more raspberries.

Serves 8–10

brown sugar bundt cake

see variations page 99

The classic bundt cake takes its name from the bundt pan in which it is baked—a ring-shaped mold with a scalloped edge. This brown sugar version drizzled with pretty white frosting is simple and delicious.

for the cake
2 sticks butter, at room
    temperature
3/4 cup light brown sugar

1/4 cup superfine sugar
4 eggs
1 2/3 cups self-rising flour
2 tbsp. milk

for the frosting
1 3/4 cups confectioners'
    sugar, sifted
2 tbsp. lemon juice

Preheat the oven to 350°F (180°C). Grease a 10-in. (25-cm.) bundt pan and dust the inside with flour.

Beat together the butter and sugars until light and creamy, then beat in the eggs one at a time. Sift the flour over the mixture and fold in. Stir in the milk, then tip batter into the prepared bundt pan, smoothing the surface with the back of the spoon.

Bake for 50 to 60 minutes, then let rest in the pan before turning out onto a wire rack to cool completely.

To make the frosting, stir together the confectioners' sugar and lemon juice to make a smooth, pourable consistency. Pour over the cooled cake, allowing it to drizzle down the sides.

Serves 8–10

variations

carrot cake

see base recipe page 63

carrot & cardamom cake
Prepare the basic recipe, using the crushed seeds of 8 cardamom pods
instead of the cinnamon.

carrot & ginger cake
Prepare the basic recipe, folding 3 chopped pieces of stem ginger in syrup
into the cake batter with the walnuts. Add 1 finely chopped piece of stem
ginger to the frosting before decorating the cake.

nut-free carrot cake
Prepare the basic recipe, omitting the walnuts.

carrot & banana cake
Prepare the basic recipe, sprinkling 1/3 cup dried banana chips over the
frosting.

carrot & beet cake
Prepare the basic recipe, substituting 1 grated beet for 1 grated carrot.

variations

madeira cake

see base recipe page 64

orange madeira cake
Prepare the basic recipe, substituting the finely grated zest of 1 orange for the lemon zest.

cherry madeira cake
Prepare the basic recipe, folding 3/4 cup cherries into the cake batter before baking.

fruity madeira cake
Prepare the basic recipe, folding 3/4 cup golden raisins into the cake batter before baking.

vanilla madeira cake
Prepare the basic recipe, substituting 1 teaspoon vanilla extract for the lemon zest.

poppyseed madeira cake
Prepare the basic recipe, folding 2 tablespoons poppyseeds into the cake batter before baking.

variations

victoria sandwich

see base recipe page 67

blueberry victoria sandwich
Prepare the basic recipe, using blueberry jelly instead of the raspberry jelly and fresh blueberries instead of the fresh raspberries.

strawberry victoria sandwich
Prepare the basic recipe, using strawberry jelly instead of the raspberry jelly and quartered or halved strawberries instead of the fresh raspberries.

simple victoria sandwich
Prepare the basic recipe, omitting the fresh raspberries and whipped cream.

black currant victoria sandwich
Prepare the basic recipe, using black currant jelly instead of the raspberry jelly and omitting the fresh fruit.

peach victoria sandwich
Prepare the basic recipe, using peach jelly instead of the raspberry jelly and fresh peach slices instead of the raspberries.

variations

dundee cake

see base recipe page 68

mixed fruit cake
Prepare the basic recipe, using only 1 1/3 cups dried vine fruits, plus 1/2 cup chopped dried dates and 1/2 cup chopped dried apricots.

spiced dundee cake
Prepare the basic recipe, adding 1 teaspoon apple pie spice with the flour.

coffee dundee cake
Prepare the basic recipe, omitting the orange zest. Add 2 teaspoons instant coffee dissolved in 1 tablespoon boiling water.

fruit cake with walnuts
Prepare the basic recipe, topping the cake with walnut halves instead of the almonds.

nut-free fruit cake
Prepare the basic recipe, omitting the almonds on top.

variations

coffee & walnut cake

see base recipe page 71

coffee & pecan cake
Prepare the basic recipe, substituting pecans for the walnuts.

coffee & macadamia cake
Prepare the basic recipe, substituting macadamia nuts for the walnuts.

coffee & hazelnut cake
Prepare the basic recipe, substituting hazelnuts for the walnuts.

coffee & brazil nut cake
Prepare the basic recipe, substituting Brazil nuts for the walnuts.

coffee cake
Prepare the basic recipe, omitting the walnuts.

pineapple upside-down cake

see base recipe page 72

orange & pineapple upside-down cake

Prepare the basic recipe, substituting the finely grated zest of 1 orange for the lemon zest.

vanilla pineapple upside-down cake

Prepare the basic recipe, replacing the lemon zest with 1 teaspoon vanilla extract.

blueberry upside-down cake

Prepare the basic recipe, substituting 1 1/3 cups fresh blueberries for the pineapple and cherries.

cranberry upside-down cake

Prepare the basic recipe, substituting 1 generous cup cranberries for the pineapple and cherries.

mango upside-down cake

Prepare the basic recipe, substituting about 1 large sliced mango for the pineapple and cherries.

variations

raspberry genoese

see base recipe page 75

mixed berry genoese
Prepare the basic recipe, using a mixture of fresh berries and strawberry halves instead of the raspberries.

peach genoese
Prepare the basic recipe, using fresh or canned peach slices instead of the raspberries.

banana genoese
Prepare the basic recipe, using slices of banana instead of the raspberries.

white chocolate & vanilla genoese
Prepare the basic recipe, adding 1 1/2 teaspoons of vanilla extract to the mix. Omit the raspberries and add 1 teaspoon vanilla extract to the whipping cream. Garnish with white chocolate curls.

cherry-chocolate genoese
Prepare the basic recipe, adding 1 tablespoon unsweetened cocoa powder to the flour. Use pitted cherries instead of the raspberries.

variations

marble cake

see base recipe page 76

pink & white marble cake
Prepare the basic recipe, omitting the cocoa powder from half of the batter
and instead tinting it with pink food coloring. Omit the frosting and dust the
cake with confectioners' sugar instead.

orange & chocolate marble cake
Prepare the basic recipe, replacing the vanilla in half of the batter with the
finely grated zest of 1 orange.

coffee & chocolate marble cake
Prepare the basic recipe, replacing the vanilla in half of the batter with
1 teaspoon instant coffee dissolved in 1/2 tablespoon boiling water.

lemon & chocolate marble cake
Prepare the basic recipe, replacing the vanilla in half of the batter with the
finely grated zest of 1 lemon.

orange poppyseed cake

see base recipe page 79

orange cake
Prepare the basic recipe, omitting the poppyseeds.

orange, ginger & poppyseed cake
Prepare the basic recipe, adding 2 chopped pieces of stem ginger in syrup
with the poppyseeds.

orange, cinnamon & poppyseed cake
Prepare the basic recipe, adding 1 teaspoon ground cinnamon with the flour.

orange poppyseed cake with crème fraîche
Prepare the basic recipe, omitting the frosting. Instead, dust the cake with
confectioners' sugar and serve with generous dollops of crème fraîche.

orange & hazelnut cake
Prepare the basic recipe, omitting the poppyseeds. Add 1/2 cup chopped
hazelnuts to the batter.

variations

devil's food cake

see base recipe page 80

devil's chocolate raspberry cake
Prepare the basic recipe, making only half the quantity of frosting. Put
1 1/3 cups fresh raspberries over the first cake layer, top with the second
cake, then swirl the frosting on top.

devil's chocolate orange cake
Add the finely grated zest of 1 orange to the cake batter. Make only half the
quantity of frosting. Spread 4 tablespoons orange curd over the first layer,
top with the second cake, and swirl the frosting on top.

devil's mocha cake
Add to the milk 2 tablespoons instant coffee dissolved in 2 tablespoons
boiling water.

devil's chocolate blueberry cake
Top the chocolate filling with 1 1/3 cup fresh blueberries before adding the
second cake layer.

devil's chocolate cherry cake
Make only half the quantity of frosting. Spread 4 tablespoons cherry jelly
over the first layer, top with the second cake, and swirl the frosting on top.

variations

dark chocolate-mocha mud cake

see base recipe page 83

chocolate–raspberry mud cake
Prepare the basic recipe, omitting the coffee and frosting. Instead, top the cake with about 1 1/3 cups fresh raspberries.

chocolate–orange mud cake
Prepare the basic recipe, omitting the coffee and adding the finely grated zest of 1 orange with the eggs instead.

chocolate mud cake
Prepare the basic recipe, omitting the coffee.

no-fuss mud cake
Prepare the basic recipe, omitting the frosting. Dust the cake with unsweetened cocoa powder and serve with heavy cream.

chocolate–cherry mud cake
Prepare the basic recipe, omitting the coffee. Instead, top the frosted cake with about 1 1/3 cups fresh or canned pitted cherries.

variations

raspberry swiss roll

see base recipe page 84

chocolate swiss roll
Prepare the basic recipe, omitting the ground almonds. Combine
2 tablespoons unsweetened cocoa powder with the flour before sifting it
into the egg mixture. Replace the raspberry jelly with chocolate spread and
the raspberries with chocolate shavings. Dust with cocoa before serving.

chocolate & raspberry swiss roll
Omit the ground almonds. Combine 2 tablespoons unsweetened cocoa
powder with the flour before sifting it into the egg mixture.

cherry & orange swiss roll
Prepare the basic recipe, folding the grated zest of 1 orange into the batter.
Use cherry jam and pitted, quartered cherries in place of the raspberries.

lemon & raspberry swiss roll
Prepare the basic recipe, using lemon curd instead of raspberry jelly.

vanilla-cream & raspberry swiss roll
Replace the raspberry jelly with whipping cream flavored with a few drops
of vanilla essence.

brown sugar bundt cake

see base recipe page 86

chocolate bundt cake
Prepare the basic recipe, omitting the brown sugar and using 1 cup superfine sugar. Sift in 3 tablespoons unsweetened cocoa powder with the flour.

lemon bundt cake
Prepare the basic recipe, omitting the brown sugar and using 1 cup superfine sugar. Add the finely grated zest of 1 lemon with the milk.

lemon & raspberry bundt cake
Prepare the recipe for lemon bundt cake above. Fill the hole in the center of the cake with fresh raspberries.

vanilla & blueberry bundt cake
Prepare the basic recipe, using 1 cup superfine sugar instead of combined brown and superfine sugars. Add 1 1/2 teaspoons vanilla extract with the milk. Instead of frosting the cake, fill the hole in the center of the cooled cake with fresh blueberries and dust the top with confectioners' sugar.

pecan bundt cake
Prepare the basic recipe, adding 1/2 cup roughly chopped pecans to the cake batter. Sprinkle the frosted cake with 1/4 cup chopped pecans.

coffee & cake

This chapter is full of recipes that go particularly

well with coffee — whether it's a light cake to serve

with morning coffee, an indulgent slice for dessert,

or a rich, sticky cake when you need a proper treat.

sticky maple pecan cake

see variations page 125

This buttery layer cake, with its fragrant flavor of maple syrup and pecans, is especially wonderful with a steaming hot cup of coffee. The bitterness of the coffee perfectly offsets the sugary sweetness of the cake.

for the cake
1 1/2 sticks butter, at room temperature
3/4 cup superfine sugar
3 eggs
scant 1 1/4 cups self-rising flour
1/2 cup pecans, roughly chopped

for the frosting
1 stick butter, at room temperature
2 tbsp. pure maple syrup
1 tbsp. milk
1 1/3 cups confectioners' sugar, sifted
pecan halves, to decorate

Preheat the oven to 350°F (180°C). Grease two 8-in. (20-cm.) round cake pans and line the bottoms with waxed paper.

Beat the butter and sugar together until pale and creamy, then beat in the eggs one at a time. Sift the flour over the egg mixture, then fold in. Add the pecans and fold in. Spoon the mixture into the prepared pans, smoothing the top with the back of the spoon. Bake for about 20 minutes until golden and a skewer inserted in the center comes out clean. Turn out onto a wire rack and let cool completely.

To decorate, beat together the butter, syrup, milk, and confectioners' sugar until smooth and creamy. Spread slightly less than half the frosting over the top of one of the cake layers. Place the second cake on top, spread with the remaining frosting, and top with pecan halves.

Serves 8

mocha chocolate cake

see variations page 126

This melt-in-the-mouth cake with its soft, mousselike center is a truly decadent treat.
Serve it with a cup of coffee when you need a pick-me-up or savor it for dessert.

9 oz. bittersweet chocolate
1 1/2 sticks butter, diced
1 cup superfine sugar
3 extra-large eggs

generous 2/3 cup all-purpose flour
2 tbsp. instant coffee dissolved in 2 tbsp. boiling
  water
heavy cream, to serve

Preheat the oven to 325°F (160°C). Grease an 8-in. (20-cm.) springform pan and line the
bottom with waxed paper.

Break the chocolate into pieces and put them in a heatproof bowl with the butter. Place the
bowl over a pan of gently simmering water and heat gently until the chocolate and butter
have melted. Remove from the heat and let cool for 5 minutes. Stir in the sugar, then beat in
the eggs, one at a time. Sift the flour over the mixture, then fold in. Stir in the coffee. Tip the
mixture into the prepared springform pan and bake for 55 minutes until firm on top, with a
slight wobble in the center. (The cake will firm as it cools.) Let the cake cool in the pan.

Carefully unmold the cake onto a serving plate and serve in wedges with heavy cream
poured over the top.

Serves 8

blueberry sour cream loaf cake

see variations page 127

The blueberries in this wonderfully soft, moist loaf cake become irresistibly juicy and tender with baking. For an extra treat, serve with a generous dollop of sour cream.

1 1/2 sticks butter, at room temperature
generous 3/4 cup superfine sugar
2 extra-large eggs
generous 3/4 cup sour cream

2 cups self-rising flour
1 tsp. ground cinnamon
1 1/3 cups fresh blueberries
confectioners' sugar, to dust (optional)

Preheat the oven to 350°F (180°C). Grease an 8 1/2 x 4 1/2-in. (2 lb.) loaf pan, and line the bottom with waxed paper.

Beat together the butter and sugar until pale and creamy, then beat in the eggs one at a time. Stir in the sour cream, then sift the flour and cinnamon over the mixture and fold in. Reserve a few blueberries (about 10) to sprinkle over the top, then fold in the remaining berries. Spoon the batter into the prepared loaf pan, smoothing the top with the back of the spoon. Sprinkle the reserved berries over the batter, pressing them down.

Bake for about 1 hour and 10 minutes, or until a skewer inserted in the center comes out clean. Let cool in the pan for about 10 minutes, then turn out on a wire rack to cool completely. Dust with confectioners' sugar before serving.

Serves 8

apple & cinnamon loaf cake

see variations page 128

This simple loaf cake layered with tangy apples makes a good choice as a no-fuss cake to serve with coffee. To transform it into more of a dessert cake, try serving with a dollop or two of sour cream and some fresh blueberries.

1 stick butter, at room temperature
3/4 cup light brown sugar
1/4 cup sour cream
1 1/2 tsp. ground cinnamon

2 extra-large eggs
1 1/2 cups self-rising flour
1 1/2 apples, peeled, cored, and sliced
4 tbsp. apricot jelly

Preheat oven to 350°F (180°C). Grease an 8 1/2 x 4 1/2-in. (2 lb.) loaf pan, and line the bottom with waxed paper.

Beat together the butter and sugar until smooth and creamy, then beat in the sour cream and cinnamon. Beat in the eggs one at a time, then sift the flour over the top and fold in.

Spoon about half the batter into the loaf pan, then top with a layer of apple slices. Spoon on the remaining batter, and top with another layer of apples, arranging the slices neatly. Bake for about 1 hour until risen and golden and a skewer inserted in the center comes out clean. Let cool in the pan for a few minutes, then turn out on a wire rack to cool.

While the cake is still warm, heat the apricot jelly in a small saucepan until it is warm, then brush over the top of the cake to glaze.

Serves 8

creamy coconut cake

see variations page 129

Rich with the flavor of coconut, this pretty, white cake is topped off perfectly with a sharp, zesty cream cheese frosting.

for the cake
1 1/4 sticks butter, at room temperature
3 tbsp. creamed coconut, at room temperature
finely grated zest of 1 lime

3/4 cup superfine sugar
3 eggs
1 cup self-rising flour
scant 2/3 cup shredded coconut

for the frosting
one 8-oz. package cream cheese
1/2 cup confectioners' sugar, sifted
1 tbsp. lime juice

Preheat the oven to 350°F (180°C). Grease two 8-in. (20-cm.) round cake pans and line the bottoms with waxed paper.

Beat together the butter, creamed coconut, lime zest, and sugar until pale and creamy. Beat in the eggs, one at a time, then sift the flour over the mixture and fold in. Stir in the shredded coconut. Spoon the cake batter into the prepared pans and spread out evenly using the back of the spoon. Bake for 20 to 25 minutes until golden brown and a skewer inserted in the center comes out clean. Turn the cakes out onto a wire rack and let cool completely.

To decorate, beat together the cream cheese, confectioners' sugar, and lime juice. Spread slightly less than half of the frosting on top of one cake layer. Place the second layer on top and swirl with the remaining frosting.

Serves 8

fragrant lavender cake

see variations page 130

Here's an oh-so-pretty cake flavored delicately with lavender. It's wonderful for serving in summer when lavender flowers are at their best.

for the cake
3/4 cup superfine sugar
1/2 tsp. dried lavender flowers
1 1/2 sticks butter, at room temperature
3 eggs
scant 1 1/4 cups self-rising flour
for the filling
7 oz. mascarpone cheese

3 tbsp. confectioners' sugar, sifted
for the frosting
1 1/2 cups confectioners' sugar, sifted
1 extra-large egg white
lilac food coloring
sprigs of fresh lavender, to decorate

Preheat the oven to 350°F (180°C). Grease two 8-in. (20-cm.) springform round cake pans, and line the bottoms with waxed paper.

Put the sugar and dried lavender flowers in a food processor and process briefly to combine. Tip into a large bowl with the butter. Beat together until pale and creamy, then beat in the eggs one at a time. Sift the flour over the mixture, then fold in.

Spoon the mixture into the prepared pans and spread out evenly using the back of the spoon. Bake for 20 to 25 minutes until golden brown and a skewer inserted in the center comes out clean. Turn the cakes out onto a wire rack and let cool completely.

To make the filling, beat together the mascarpone and sugar. Spread it over one of the cooled cakes. Top with the second cake.

To make the frosting, beat the confectioners' sugar into the egg white until thick and creamy. Add a few drops of food coloring to make the frosting a pretty lavender color. Pour over the cake, and let stand a few hours to firm up. Garnish with fresh lavender sprigs.

Serves 8

creamy pistachio cake

see variations page 131

This tender, light cake sandwiched with a rich lemon cream is delicious with a cup of coffee, but it's so pretty that it's perfect for a special occasion as well.

for the cake
1/2 cup shelled pistachio nuts
1 1/2 sticks butter, at room
    temperature
3/4 cup superfine sugar
3 eggs

1 cup self-rising flour
for the filling
2 1/2 tbsp. lemon curd
1/2 cup sour cream
for the frosting
1 egg white

scant 1 1/4 cups confectioners'
    sugar, sifted
3/4 tsp. lemon juice
green food coloring
white sugared flowers and
    silver dragées*, to decorate

Preheat the oven to 350°F (180°C). Grease two 8-in. (20-cm.) round cake pans, and line the bottoms with waxed paper. Finely grind the pistachio nuts in a food processor, then set aside.

Beat together the butter and sugar until pale and fluffy. Beat in the eggs one at a time. Stir in the ground pistachios, then sift the flour on top and fold in. Spoon the cake batter into the prepared pans and spread out evenly using the back of the spoon. Bake for 20 to 25 minutes until golden brown and the cake springs back when pressed lightly with the tips of your fingers. Turn the cakes out onto a wire rack and let cool completely. To make the filling, stir together the lemon curd and sour cream until thoroughly combined. Spread evenly over one cake layer, then top with the second layer. Gradually whisk the confectioners' sugar into the egg white until thick and glossy, then beat in the lemon juice. Add a few drops of food coloring to make the frosting a pretty shade of pistachio green, then pour it over the cake. Decorate with sugared flowers and dragées, and serve.

Serves 8
*silver dragées are illegal in some states so only purchase them from reputable stores

frosted angel food cake

see variations page 133

This light-as-air, snowy-white cake is an American classic and great served with coffee. It's traditionally baked in a tube pan and served in slices.

for the cake
3/4 cup all-purpose flour
1 generous cup superfine sugar
10 egg whites
1 tsp. cream of tartar
1/2 tsp. vanilla extract

for the frosting
1/2 cup superfine sugar
4 tbsp. water
2 egg whites
2 tsp. corn syrup
1/2 tsp. vanilla extract
fresh strawberries, to serve

Preheat the oven to 350°F (180°C). In a large bowl, sift together the flour and half the sugar three times until very light. Set aside.

In a clean bowl, whisk the egg whites with the cream of tartar until stiff, then gradually whisk in the remaining 1/2 cup sugar until thick and glossy. Whisk in the vanilla extract.

Sift half the flour and sugar mixture over the egg whites, then fold it in. Repeat with the remaining flour and sugar mixture. Spoon the batter into a nonstick ring-shaped cake pan with a hollow tubular center, or a 10-in. (25-cm.) ring mold. Bake for about 40 minutes, or until a skewer inserted into the cake comes out clean. Turn the cake out onto a wire rack and let cool.

To make the frosting, put the sugar in a small pan with the 4 tbsp. water. Heat, stirring, until the sugar dissolves, then boil until the temperature reaches 240°F (115°C).

In a clean bowl, whisk the egg whites until very stiff, then pour the hot syrup into the egg whites in a thin stream, whisking continuously. Add the corn syrup and vanilla. Continue whisking until the frosting is cooled, then spread over the cake. Serve with strawberries.

Serves 8

apricot & hazelnut loaf cake

see variations page 133

Sweet, nutty, and rich with the intense flavor of apricot, this simple loaf cake is perfect for any occasion. Bake it when you have guests for coffee, or just enjoy it as an everyday treat.

2/3 cup roasted hazelnuts
1 1/2 sticks butter, at room temperature
1/2 cup superfine sugar
1/4 cup light brown sugar
2 eggs

finely grated zest of 1 lemon
scant 1 1/4 cups self-rising flour
1 tsp. baking powder
2/3 cup dried apricots, chopped

Preheat the oven to 350°F (180°C). Grease an 8 1/2 x 4 1/2-in. (2lb.) loaf pan, and line the bottom with waxed paper.

Put the hazelnuts in a food processor and process until coarsely ground, then set aside.

Beat together the butter and sugars until smooth and creamy, then beat in the eggs one at a time. Stir in the lemon zest, then sift the flour and baking powder over the batter. Add the ground nuts and fold together until well mixed. Fold in the apricots.

Spoon the mixture into the prepared loaf pan, smoothing out the top with the back of the spoon. Bake for 50 minutes to 1 hour or until a skewer inserted in the center comes out clean. Let cool in the pan for about 10 minutes, then transfer to a wire rack to cool completely.

Serves 8

honey & pine nut cake

see variations page 134

Sweet, dense, and stickily chewy, this simple cake is fabulous at any time of day. You could even serve it warm for dessert with whipped cream or ice cream.

for the cake
2 sticks butter, diced
1/2 cup clear honey
1/3 cup light corn syrup
1/2 cup light brown sugar
3 extra-large eggs

2/3 cup toasted pine nuts
2 cups self-rising flour
for the topping
1/4 cup toasted pine nuts
4 tbsp. clear honey

Preheat the oven to 325°F (160°C). Grease an 8-in. (20-cm.) round cake pan and line the bottom with waxed paper.

Put the butter, honey, corn syrup, and brown sugar in a saucepan. Heat gently over low heat, stirring, until the butter has melted and the mixture is thoroughly combined. Set aside to cool for about 10 minutes. Beat in the eggs, one at a time. Reserve 2 tbsp. of the pine nuts and stir the rest into the mixture. Sift the flour over the mixture, then stir to combine. Pour batter into the prepared cake pan. Sprinkle the reserved pine nuts on top.

Bake cake for about 1 hour and 10 minutes until a skewer inserted in the center comes out clean. Remove the cake from the oven and let it cool in the pan for about 5 minutes before turning out onto a wire rack.

While the cake is warm, prepare the topping. Put the pine nuts and honey in a pan and warm gently until runny. Pour over the cake, spreading the mixture evenly over the top.

Serves 8

plum streusel cake

see variations page 135

The combination of delicately flavored vanilla cake with tangy, juicy plums and nutty hazelnut streusel is divine in this simple coffee cake. Serve in big wedges with a fork.

for the topping
1/2 cup hazelnuts
generous 2/3 cup all-purpose flour
1/2 stick butter, cubed
1/4 cup demerara sugar

for the cake
1 stick butter, at room temperature
1/2 cup superfine sugar
2 eggs

generous 2/3 cup self-rising flour
1/2 teaspoon vanilla extract
about 1 1/2 fresh, ripe plums, unpeeled, halved, and pitted

Preheat the oven to 375°F (190°C). Grease an 8-in. (20-cm.) springform cake pan and line the bottom with waxed paper.

First make the topping. Process half the nuts in a food processor until finely ground. Chop the remaining nuts. Set aside. In a clean bowl, rub together the flour, ground hazelnuts, and butter until the mixture resembles bread crumbs. Stir in the sugar and chopped nuts. Set aside.

To make the cake, beat together the butter and sugar until pale and creamy, then beat in the eggs one at a time. Sift the flour over the mixture, then fold in. Stir in the vanilla. Spoon the mixture into the cake pan, smoothing the top with the back of the spoon. Top with the plum halves, cut-side facing downward. Sprinkle the topping over the plums and bake for about 1 hour and 20 minutes until a skewer inserted into the center of the cake comes out clean. Let cool completely in the pan before serving.

Serves 8

orange syrup cake

see variations page 136

This moist sticky cake is best served with a fork. For a wicked twist, serve it with a generous dollop of crème fraîche or drenched in whipping cream.

for the cake
1 orange
1 1/2 sticks butter, at room temperature
3/4 cup superfine sugar

3 eggs
scant 1 1/4 cups self-rising flour
1/2 tsp. baking soda
4 tbsp. ground almonds

for the syrup
finely grated zest and juice of 1 orange
1/4 cup superfine sugar

Preheat the oven to 375°F (190°C). Grease a 10-in. (23-cm.) round cake pan and line the bottom with waxed paper.

Finely grate the zest from the orange and set aside. Cut the peel and white pith from the orange, then roughly chop the flesh, removing any seeds. Blend the flesh in a food processor until smooth. Set aside.

Beat together the butter and sugar until pale and creamy, then beat in the eggs one at a time. Stir in the orange purée and grated zest, then sift the flour and baking soda over the bowl, and fold in. Fold in the ground almonds. Bake for 25 to 30 minutes until risen and golden and a skewer inserted in the center comes out clean. Let cool in the pan for about 10 minutes, then turn out on a wire rack to cool completely.

To make the syrup, put the orange zest and juice in a small pan with the sugar. Warm gently, stirring, until the sugar has dissolved.

Bring to a vigorous boil, then remove from the heat. Pour the syrup over the warm cake and let stand for at least 30 minutes before serving.

Serves 8–10

rhubarb upside-down cake

see variations page 137

Tart rhubarb makes a fabulously fruity, gooey topping for the golden sponge base of this cake. As it cooks, the rhubarb turns a gorgeous pink that's impossible to resist.

generous 1/2 lb. fresh rhubarb, cut into about
    1/4-in. (7-mm.) thick slices
3 tbsp. superfine sugar
3/4 stick butter, at room temperature
1 1/4 cups superfine sugar

2 extra-large eggs
3 tbsp. ground almonds
scant 1 cup self-rising flour
crème fraîche, to serve

Preheat the oven to 350°F (180°C). Grease an 8-in. (20-cm.) round cake pan and line the bottom with waxed paper.

Toss the sliced rhubarb in 3 tbsp. sugar to coat thoroughly. Arrange the rhubarb over the bottom of the pan.

Beat the butter and 1 1/4 cups sugar until pale and creamy, then beat in the eggs one at a time. Stir in the almonds, then sift the flour over the mixture and fold in. Spoon onto the rhubarb and spread out evenly.

Bake for about 40 minutes until risen and golden and a skewer inserted in the center comes out clean. Let cool in the pan for about 5 minutes, then turn onto a wire rack to cool. Serve warm or cold with crème fraîche.

Serves 8

sticky maple pecan cake

see base recipe page 101

sticky maple pecan & coffee cake
Prepare the basic recipe. Dissolve 2 teaspoons instant coffee in 1 tablespoon boiling water, then fold it into the cake batter before baking. For the frosting, replace the milk with 2 teaspoons instant coffee dissolved in 1 tablespoon boiling water.

sticky maple pecan & chocolate chip cake
Prepare the basic recipe, folding 1/2 cup semisweet chocolate chips into the cake with the nuts.

sticky maple walnut cake
Prepare the basic recipe, substituting walnuts for the pecans.

sticky maple hazelnut cake
Prepare the basic recipe, substituting hazelnuts for the pecans.

sticky maple brazil nut cake
Prepare the basic recipe, substituting Brazil nuts for the pecans.

variations

mocha chocolate cake

see base recipe page 102

dark chocolate cake
Prepare the basic recipe, omitting the coffee.

chocolate & orange cake
Prepare the basic recipe, replacing the coffee with the finely grated zest of 1 orange.

chocolate & vanilla cake
Prepare the basic recipe, substituting 2 teaspoons vanilla extract for the coffee.

chocolate cake with strawberries
Prepare the basic recipe, omitting the coffee. Serve with fresh strawberries and heavy cream.

chocolate & amaretto cake
Prepare the basic recipe, replacing the coffee with 2 tablespoons Amaretto liqueur.

variations

blueberry sour cream loaf cake

see base recipe page 105

blueberry & lime loaf cake
Prepare the basic recipe, omitting the ground cinnamon and adding the finely grated zest of 1 lime with the butter and sugar.

blueberry & lemon loaf cake
Prepare the basic recipe, omitting the cinnamon and adding the finely grated zest of 1 lemon with the butter and sugar. Drizzle with lemon frosting rather than dusting with confectioners' sugar.

spiced blueberry sour cream loaf cake
Prepare the basic recipe, replacing the ground cinnamon with 1 teaspoon apple pie spice.

blueberry & vanilla loaf cake
Prepare the basic recipe, omitting the cinnamon and adding 1 teaspoon vanilla extract with the eggs.

blueberry & rosewater cake
Prepare the basic recipe, omitting the cinnamon and adding 2 teaspoons rosewater with the eggs.

variations

apple & cinnamon loaf cake

see base recipe page 106

apple & brown sugar loaf cake
Prepare the basic recipe, omitting the cinnamon.

pear & cinnamon loaf cake
Prepare the basic recipe, using 1 1/2 pears instead of the apples.

spiced apple loaf cake
Prepare the basic recipe, substituting apple pie spice for the cinnamon.

apple & orange loaf cake
Prepare the basic recipe, substituting the finely grated zest of
1 orange for the cinnamon.

creamy coconut cake

see base recipe page 109

creamy coconut cake with blueberries
Prepare the basic recipe, scattering 1 1/2 cups fresh blueberries over the frosted cake.

creamy coconut cake with strawberries
Prepare the basic recipe, scattering the top of the frosted cake with 1 1/3 cups fresh strawberries, halved or quartered if large.

creamy coconut cake with cherries
Prepare the basic recipe, scattering 3/4 cup pitted fresh cherries over the frosted cake.

creamy coconut cake with fresh mango
Prepare the basic recipe, decorating the top of the frosted cake with slices of fresh mango.

lemony coconut cake
Prepare the basic recipe, substituting the finely grated zest of 1 lemon for the lime zest and substitute lemon juice for the lime juice.

variations

fragrant lavender cake

see base recipe page 110

lavender & blueberry cake
Sprinkle 1 3/4 cups fresh blueberries over the mascarpone filling. Omit the frosting and simply dust the top with confectioners' sugar.

lavender & raspberry cake
Prepare the basic recipe, but replace the mascarpone filling with 3 to 4 tablespoons raspberry jelly between the cake layers.

rose & cherry cake
Omit the lavender and add 1 tablespoon rosewater to the batter. Replace the mascarpone filling with 3 to 4 tablespoons cherry jelly. Use pink color in the frosting instead of lilac, and decorate using rose petals instead of lavender.

lavender & strawberry cake
Replace the mascarpone filling with 3 to 4 tablespoons strawberry jelly between the cake layers. Serve with fresh strawberries.

orange blossom cake
Omit the lavender and add 1 teaspoon orange flower water to the batter. Use orange color in the frosting instead of lilac, and decorate with orange blossom rather than sprigs of lavender.

variations

creamy pistachio cake

see base recipe page 113

simple pistachio cake
Prepare the basic cake recipe. Instead of the lemon cream filling, spread 3 to 4 tablespoons lemon curd between the cake layers. Omit the frosting, and dust the top with confectioners' sugar.

pistachio cake with orange cream
Prepare the basic recipe, substituting orange curd for the lemon curd.

creamy walnut cake
Prepare the basic recipe, using walnuts instead of pistachios. Omit the green food coloring from the frosting, and decorate with walnut halves instead of sugared flowers.

creamy hazelnut cake
Prepare the basic recipe, using hazelnuts instead of pistachios. Omit the green food coloring from the frosting, and decorate with hazelnuts instead of sugared flowers.

variations

frosted angel food cake

see base recipe page 114

angel food cake with chocolate sauce
Prepare the basic recipe, omitting the frosting. Instead, chop up 7 ounces semisweet chocolate and warm gently in a saucepan with a generous 3/4 cup whipping cream. Stir until the chocolate is nearly melted, then remove from the heat and stir until smooth and thick. Pour over the cake and serve.

lemon angel food cake
Prepare the basic recipe, substituting the finely grated zest of 1 lemon for the vanilla extract.

orange angel food cake
Prepare the basic recipe, substituting the finely grated zest of 1 orange for the vanilla extract.

pistachio angel food cake
Prepare the basic recipe, sprinkling the frosted cake with chopped pistachios.

hazelnut angel food cake
Prepare the basic recipe, sprinkling the frosted cake with chopped hazelnuts.

apricot & hazelnut loaf cake

see base recipe page 117

fig & hazelnut loaf cake
Prepare the basic recipe, using dried figs instead of the apricots.

golden raisin & hazelnut loaf cake
Prepare the basic recipe, using golden raisins instead of the chopped apricots.

apricot & almond loaf cake
Prepare the basic recipe, using ground almonds instead of the ground hazelnuts.

orange, apricot & hazelnut loaf cake
Prepare the basic recipe, using the finely grated zest of 1 orange instead of the lemon zest.

date & hazelnut loaf cake
Prepare the basic recipe, using pitted dates instead of the apricots.

honey & pine nut cake

see base recipe page 118

honey & almond cake
Prepare the basic recipe, replacing the pine nuts with slivered almonds.

honey, ginger & pine nut cake
Prepare the basic recipe, adding 1 teaspoon ground ginger to the butter, sugar, and corn syrup in the saucepan. Stir in 2 chopped pieces stem ginger in syrup with the pine nuts.

honey, orange & pine nut cake
Prepare the basic recipe, adding the finely grated zest of 1 orange with the pine nuts.

honey, lemon & pine nut cake
Prepare the basic recipe, adding the finely grated zest of 1 lemon with the pine nuts.

honey, cinnamon & pine nut cake
Prepare the basic recipe, adding 1 teaspoon ground cinnamon to the butter, sugar, and corn syrup in the saucepan.

variations

plum streusel cake

see base recipe page 121

apricot streusel cake
Prepare the basic recipe, using fresh apricots instead of the plums.

almond & plum streusel cake
Prepare the basic recipe, using almonds instead of the hazelnuts.

orange & plum streusel cake
Prepare the basic recipe, using the finely grated zest of 1 orange instead of the vanilla extract.

lemon & plum streusel cake
Prepare the basic recipe, using the finely grated zest of 1 lemon instead of the vanilla extract.

walnut & plum streusel cake
Prepare the basic recipe, using walnuts instead of the hazelnuts.

orange syrup cake

see base recipe page 122

orange & hazelnut syrup cake
Prepare the basic recipe, using ground hazelnuts instead of the ground almonds.

orange & lemon syrup cake
Prepare the basic recipe, substituting the finely grated zest and juice of 1 lemon for the orange in the syrup.

simple orange cake
Make the basic recipe, omitting the syrup. Serve dusted with confectioners' sugar instead.

nutty orange syrup cake
Prepare the basic recipe. Stir 1/3 cup chopped almonds into the syrup before pouring it over the cake.

rhubarb upside-down cake

see base recipe page 124

rhubarb & vanilla upside-down cake
Prepare the basic recipe, omitting the almonds and adding 1 teaspoon
vanilla extract instead.

rhubarb & lemon upside-down cake
Prepare the basic recipe, adding the finely grated zest of 1 lemon with the
almonds.

rhubarb & orange upside-down cake
Prepare the basic recipe, adding the finely grated zest of 1 orange with the
almonds.

spiced rhubarb upside-down cake
Prepare the basic recipe, adding 1 teaspoon apple pie spice with the ground
almonds.

rhubarb & ginger upside-down cake
Prepare the basic recipe, adding 3 chopped pieces of stem ginger in syrup
with the ground almonds, and 1 teaspoon ground ginger with the flour.

creamy cheesecakes

Whether you like them fresh and fruity, sharp and

tangy, baked or chilled, or rich and dark, there's a

cheesecake here for everyone. In fact, there are so

many recipes, you could bake a different cheesecake

every week of the year.

new york cheesecake

see variations page 162

This simple cheesecake, flavored with lemon and vanilla and topped with a snowy white layer of sour cream, is an all-time classic.

for the cake
2 cups finely ground graham
    cracker crumbs
1 stick butter, melted
18 oz. cream cheese
2/3 cup superfine sugar

1 tsp. cornstarch
generous 3/4 cup sour cream
3 extra-large eggs
1 1/2 tsp. vanilla extract
finely grated zest and juice of
    1 lemon

for the topping
1 1/4 cups sour cream
2 tbsp. superfine sugar

Grease an 8-in. (20-cm.) round springform cake pan. Stir crumbs into melted butter, then pour mixture into prepared cake pan. Press crumbs into base and about halfway up sides of pan. Chill for 30 minutes until firm. Wrap base and sides of pan in two layers of foil.

Meanwhile, preheat oven to 350°F (180°C). Beat the cream cheese until soft, then beat in the sugar and cornstarch, followed by the sour cream. Beat in eggs one at a time, then stir in the vanilla and lemon zest and juice. Pour the filling over the graham cracker base, and tap the sides of the pan to level the surface. Put the springform pan in a roasting pan. Pour boiling water into the roasting pan to about 1 to 1 1/2 inches deep. Bake cheesecake for about 40 minutes.

Combine the sour cream and sugar for the topping and spoon over the cheesecake. Return cheesecake to oven for about 10 minutes, then remove and let cool completely. Chill for at least 4 hours or overnight. Carefully unmold before serving.

Serves 8

honey & ricotta cheesecake

see variations page 163

This sweet, honeyed cheesecake with a pine nut base retains the wonderfully distinctive texture of ricotta with the added creaminess of mascarpone.

1 2/3 cups finely ground
   graham cracker crumbs
1/2 stick butter, melted
1/2 cup toasted pine nuts
1 cup ricotta cheese

1 cup mascarpone cheese
5 tbsp. sour cream
3/4 cup clear honey
2 tsp. cornstarch, dissolved in
   1 tsp. cold water

finely grated zest of 1 lemon
4 eggs, beaten

Grease an 8-in. (20-cm.) round springform cake pan. Stir crumbs into the melted butter along with pine nuts. Spread crumbs over the base and about halfway up the sides of the pan, pressing down firmly. Chill for 30 minutes. Wrap pan in two layers of foil.

Meanwhile, preheat oven to 325°F (170°C). Beat together the ricotta and mascarpone until smooth and creamy, then beat in the sour cream, honey, lemon zest, and cornstarch, followed by the eggs.

Pour the filling over the crumb base and place the cake pan in a roasting pan. Pour in boiling water to reach about 1 to 1 1/2 inches up the sides of the cake pan. Cook for about 1 hour and 25 minutes until set (but still with a wobble in the center). Transfer pan to a wire rack to cool completely, then chill overnight before carefully unmolding and serving.

Serves 8

creamy lime & blueberry cheesecake

see variations page 164

Tangy with lime, this rich and creamy cheesecake is studded with blueberries, which give it a fabulous texture.

1 2/3 cups finely ground
   graham cracker crumbs
1/2 stick butter, melted
1 lb. (two 8-oz. packages)
   cream cheese

3/4 cup superfine sugar
2 tsp. cornstarch
2/3 cup sour cream
3 extra-large eggs

finely grated zest and juice of
   1 or 2 limes
1 cup fresh blueberries, plus
   1 1/4 cups to decorate

Grease a 10-in. (23-cm.) round springform cake pan. Stir the crumbs into the melted butter, then spread over the bottom of the prepared pan, pressing down to make an even base. Chill for 30 minutes. Wrap the base and sides of pan in two layers of foil to make a watertight seal.

Preheat oven to 350°F (180°C). Beat the cream cheese until creamy, then beat in the sugar and cornstarch. Stir in the sour cream until smooth and creamy, then beat in the eggs followed by the lime zest and juice. Fold in 1 cup blueberries. Pour filling into the cake pan, tapping the sides of the pan to level the surface.

Place pan in a roasting pan and pour boiling water around it to about 1 to 1 1/2 inches deep. Bake for 45 minutes until set (but still with a wobble in the middle). Let cool, then chill for at least 4 hours or overnight. To serve, carefully unmold and top with remaining fresh blueberries.

Serves 8–10

white chocolate cheesecake

see variations page 165

This deeply filled cheesecake is sweet and rich with a mousselike texture and an intense white chocolate flavor. Perfect for any occasion.

1 2/3 cups finely ground graham cracker crumbs
1/2 stick butter, melted
3 tbsp. bittersweet chocolate chips
6 oz. white chocolate
14 oz. cream cheese

3/4 cup superfine sugar
2/3 cup crème fraîche
1 tsp. vanilla extract
3 extra-large eggs, separated
unsweetened cocoa powder, for dusting

Grease an 8-in. (20-cm.) round springform cake pan. Stir crumbs into melted butter. Spread the buttered crumbs over the bottom of the prepared pan, pressing down to make an even base. Sprinkle with the chocolate chips, and press them gently into the crumbs. Chill for 30 minutes. Wrap the base and sides of the pan in two layers of foil to make a watertight seal.

Preheat oven to 350°F (180°C). Break the white chocolate into a heatproof bowl set over a pan of barely simmering water. Let the chocolate melt slowly, then remove the pan from the heat and let it cool for about 10 minutes.

Beat the cream cheese until soft, then beat in the sugar followed by the crème fraîche and vanilla. Beat until smooth and creamy. Beat in the egg yolks one at a time, then fold in the cooled white chocolate. Whisk the egg whites in a separate bowl until they form soft peaks, then add to the chocolate mixture and fold in.

Pour the mixture over the biscuit base and smooth the surface. Bake for about 50 minutes until firm (but still with a wobble in the middle). Remove pan from oven and let cool, then chill for at least 4 hours. To serve, carefully unmold and dust with unsweetened cocoa.

Serves 8–10

cappuccino cheesecake

see variations page 166

Sweet and creamy with the distinctive bitter flavor of coffee, this luscious cheesecake makes a fabulous dessert or a treat to serve with coffee.

1 2/3 cups finely ground
   graham cracker crumbs
1/2 stick butter, melted
20 oz. mascarpone
5 tbsp. crème fraîche

4 tbsp. instant coffee, dissolved
   in 4 tbsp. boiling water
1/2 cup superfine sugar, plus
   1 1/2 tbsp. for the topping
4 eggs, beaten

1 cup sour cream
unsweetened cocoa powder, for
   dusting

Grease an 8-in. (20-cm.) round springform cake pan. Stir crumbs into melted butter. Spread the mixture over bottom of prepared pan, pressing down to make an even base. Chill for 30 minutes until firm.

Meanwhile, preheat the oven to 350°F (180°C). Beat together the mascarpone and crème fraîche until smooth, then stir in the coffee and 1/2 cup sugar. Stir in the eggs until well mixed. Wrap the base and sides of the springform pan in two layers of foil, then pour in the mascarpone mixture. Place pan in a roasting pan and pour water around it to reach half to two-thirds of the way up the sides. Bake for about 50 minutes until set but still soft.

Meanwhile, stir the remaining 1 1/2 tbsp. sugar into the sour cream. Remove the cheesecake from the oven and gently spoon the sour cream on top, spreading it out evenly. Return pan to oven for 10 minutes, then remove and let cool. Chill for at least 4 hours or overnight. To serve, carefully unmold and dust with cocoa powder.

Serves 8

black currant cheesecake

see variations page 167

Dark, tangy black currant compote makes a wonderful contrast of flavor and color in this luxurious cheesecake. You can use fresh or frozen black currants.

for the cake
1 2/3 cups finely ground
    graham cracker crumbs
1/2 stick butter, melted
18 oz. cream cheese

1 cup sour cream
3/4 cup superfine sugar
2 tsp. vanilla extract
3 extra-large eggs

for the topping
about 3 1/2 cups black
    currants
1 tbsp. water
about 4 tbsp. superfine sugar

Grease a 10-in. (23-cm.) round springform cake pan. Stir crumbs into melted butter. Spread the buttered crumbs over the bottom of the prepared pan, pressing down to make an even base. Chill for 30 minutes, then wrap the base and sides of pan in two layers of foil.

Preheat oven to 350°F (180°C). Beat the cream cheese with the sour cream, sugar, and vanilla. Beat in the eggs one at a time until the mixture is smooth. Pour the mixture over the biscuit base.

Put the cake pan into a roasting pan, then pour boiling water around the pan to about 1 to 1 1/2 inches. Bake for about 50 minutes until set (but still with a wobble in the center). Remove from oven and let cool.

To make the topping, put the black currants, water, and sugar in a saucepan. Slowly bring to a boil, stirring occasionally. Simmer until the currants are just tender. Remove from the heat, check the flavor, and add a little more sugar if needed. Let cool.

Pour the cooled topping over the cooled cheesecake and chill for at least 4 hours or overnight. Carefully unmold before serving.

Serves 8–10

zesty lemon cheesecake

see variations page 168

Lower in fat than some classic cheesecakes, this recipe combines cream cheese with fat-free fromage frais to make a cheesecake with a light, creamy, almost mousselike filling with a fresh, lemony zing.

5 oz. gingersnaps
1/2 stick butter, melted
14 oz. low-fat cream cheese
7 oz. fat-free fromage frais or fromage blanc
3 tbsp. sour cream

3/4 cup superfine sugar
2 tsp. cornstarch
3 extra-large eggs
finely grated zest of 2 lemons
juice of 1 lemon

Grease an 8-in. (20-cm.) round springform cake pan. Put the gingersnaps in a food processor and process to make fine crumbs. Stir the crumbs into the butter. Tip the mixture into the prepared pan and spread over the base, pressing down firmly. Chill for 30 minutes, then wrap the pan in two layers of foil to make a watertight seal.

Preheat oven to 350°F (180°C). Beat the cream cheese until soft, then beat in the fromage frais, sour cream, sugar, and cornstarch until smooth and creamy. Beat in the eggs one at a time, then stir in the lemon juice and zest. Pour the mixture over the crumb base and tap the pan to level the surface.

Place the cake pan in a roasting pan and pour boiling water around it to about 1 to 1 1/2 inches. Bake for 50 minutes until set (but still with a wobble in the center). Remove from oven, let cool in pan, then chill for at least 4 hours or overnight. Carefully unmold before serving.

Serves 8

strawberry vanilla cheesecake

see variations page 169

Unlike a classic baked cheesecake, this creamy, intensely flavored cheesecake relies on gelatin to set it. Serve with fresh strawberries on the side.

1 2/3 cups finely ground graham cracker crumbs
3/4 stick butter, melted
9 oz. cream cheese
3/4 cup superfine sugar
scant 1 cup whipping cream
1 lb. fresh, ripe strawberries, hulled

juice of 1 lemon
1 tsp. vanilla extract
4 tbsp. boiling water
1 1/2 tbsp. unflavored gelatin
15 whole strawberries to decorate

Grease an 8-in. (20-cm.) round springform cake pan. Stir crumbs into melted butter, then spread over the bottom of the prepared pan, pressing down to make an even base. Chill for 30 minutes. Beat the cream cheese and sugar until smooth and creamy. In a separate bowl, whip the cream until it forms soft peaks. Set both bowls aside. Put the strawberries in a food processor and blend to a purée, then strain to remove the seeds. Stir in the lemon juice and vanilla, then gradually beat into the cream cheese mixture until smooth.

Put the boiling water in a small bowl, sprinkle the gelatin on top, and let it stand to dissolve. Stir well before stirring it into the strawberry-cream cheese mixture. Fold about one-quarter of this mixture into the whipped cream, then fold in the rest. Pour over the graham cracker base and chill for at least 3 hours until set. To serve, carefully unmold and decorate with whole strawberries.

Serves 8

dark chocolate cheesecake

see variations page 170

This wonderful cheesecake just melts in the mouth and makes a fabulous dessert or an extra-indulgent afternoon treat. It's rich, creamy, and with just the perfect hit of bitter chocolate.

2 cups finely ground graham cracker crumbs
2 tsp. unsweetened cocoa powder, plus extra
    for dusting
3/4 stick butter, melted
7 oz. semisweet chocolate

14 oz. cream cheese
1 cup sour cream
3/4 cup superfine sugar
2 tsp. cornstarch
3 extra-large eggs

Grease an 8-in. (20-cm.) round springform cake pan. Mix crumbs, cocoa powder, and melted butter. Press crumb mixture over the bottom and about halfway up the sides of the cake pan. Chill for 30 minutes. Wrap the pan in two sheets of aluminum foil. Preheat the oven to 320°F (160°C). Break the semisweet chocolate into a heatproof bowl, then set the bowl over a pan of barely simmering water to melt. Remove from the heat, and set aside to cool.

Beat the cream cheese until soft, then beat in the sour cream, sugar, and cornstarch. Beat in the eggs one at a time, then fold in the cooled, melted chocolate. Pour the mixture into the cake pan and level out. Place the cake pan in a roasting pan and pour boiling water around it to about 1 to 1 1/2 inches deep. Bake for about 50 minutes until set (but still with a wobble in the center). Remove from the oven and let cool completely, then chill for at least 4 hours or overnight. To serve, carefully unmold and dust with cocoa powder.

Serves 8

amaretto cheesecake

see variations page 171

Sweet and creamy, with a distinctive texture provided by the crushed amaretti in the filling, this luscious almond-flavored cheesecake offers something of an adult dessert that's just great for entertaining.

for the cake
7 oz. amaretti cookies
3/4 stick butter, melted
7 oz. cream cheese

9 oz. mascarpone cheese
scant 1/2 cup crème fraîche
2/3 cup superfine sugar
2 tsp. cornstarch, dissolved in
    2 tsp. water

6 tbsp. Amaretto liqueur
3 extra-large eggs
crushed amaretti, to decorate

Grease an 8-in. (20-cm.) round springform cake pan. Put 5 oz. of the cookies in a food processor and process into crumbs. Stir crumbs into melted butter, then press buttered crumbs evenly over the base of the pan. Chill for 30 minutes, then wrap pan in two layers of aluminum foil.

Meanwhile, preheat the oven to 350°F (180°C). Beat the cream cheese and mascarpone until soft, then beat in the crème fraîche, sugar, and cornstarch until smooth and creamy. Beat in the Amaretto, followed by the eggs one at a time. Beat smooth. Put the remaining cookies in a plastic bag and crush roughly with a rolling pin. Add the crumbs to the cream cheese mixture and fold in.

Pour the filling over the crumb base and tap the sides of the pan to level the surface. Place the cake pan in a roasting pan and pour boiling water around it to about 1 to 1 1/2 inches deep.

Bake for about 50 minutes until firm (but still with a wobble in the center). Let cool, then chill for at least 4 hours or overnight. To serve, carefully unmold and decorate with more crushed amaretti.

Serves 8

mango cheesecake

see variations page 172

Look for really well-flavored mangoes for this simple chilled cheesecake. The combination of cream cheese with Greek yogurt creates a meltingly mouthwatering filling.

5 oz. gingersnaps
3/4 stick butter, melted
2 large ripe mangoes, pitted and peeled
juice of 2 limes
7 oz. cream cheese

3/4 cup superfine sugar
generous 3/4 cup Greek yogurt
4 tbsp. boiling water
1 1/2 tbsp. unflavored gelatin

Grease an 8-in. (20-cm.) round springform cake pan. Put the gingersnaps in a food processor and process to make fine crumbs. Stir into the butter, then tip into the prepared cake pan and press down over the base. Chill for 30 minutes.

Put the mango flesh in a blender and blend to a smooth purée. Stir in the lime juice and set aside.

In a separate bowl, beat the cream cheese and sugar together, then beat in the yogurt, followed by the mango purée.

Put the boiling water in a bowl and sprinkle the gelatin on top. Let dissolve, then stir thoroughly before stirring into the mango mixture. Pour the filling into the cake pan and chill overnight, or for at least 3 hours until set. Carefully unmold before serving.

Serves 8

rum raisin cheesecake

see variations page 173

Rum and raisins is a classic pairing in desserts, and nowhere is it better than in this easy-to-make cheesecake. For best results, take the cheesecake out of the fridge about 20 minutes before serving.

4 tbsp. rum
1/2 cup raisins
2 cups finely ground graham cracker crumbs
7 tbsp. butter, melted
18 oz. cream cheese

1/2 cup crème fraîche
3/4 cup superfine sugar
1 tsp. cornstarch
1 tsp. vanilla extract
2 eggs

Pour the rum over the raisins and let soak overnight.

Grease a 10-in. (23-cm.) springform cake pan. Stir crumbs into the melted butter. Spread the mixture over the bottom of the cake pan, pressing down to make an even base. Chill for 30 minutes until firm. Wrap the pan with 2 layers of aluminum foil.

Preheat the oven to 350°F (180°C). Beat together the cream cheese, crème fraîche, sugar, and cornstarch until creamy, then beat in the vanilla and eggs. Fold in the raisins and soaking liquid. Pour the mixture over the crumb base.

Bake for 50 to 55 minutes until the cheesecake is set (but still with a wobble in the center). Remove from the oven and let cool completely, then chill overnight, or for at least 3 hours. Carefully unmold before serving.

Serves 8–10

variations

new york cheesecake

see base recipe page 139

raspberry new york cheesecake
Prepare the basic recipe. Top the chilled baked cheesecake with fresh
raspberries before serving.

gingersnap new york cheesecake
Prepare the basic recipe, using gingersnap crumbs instead of graham
crackers. Top the chilled baked cheesecake with sliced fresh strawberries
before serving.

orange & dark chocolate new york cheesecake
Prepare the basic recipe, adding the grated zest of 1 orange in place of the
vanilla essence. Decorate the chilled cheesecake with dark chocolate curls.

fresh fig new york cheesecake
Prepare the basic recipe. Top the chilled baked cheesecake with slices of
fresh figs before serving.

blueberry new york cheesecake
Prepare the basic recipe. Top the chilled baked cheesecake with fresh
blueberries before serving.

honey & ricotta cheesecake

see base recipe page 140

ginger, honey & ricotta cheesecake
Prepare the basic recipe, replacing the graham cracker crumbs with gingersnap crumbs. Fold 2 chopped pieces of stem ginger in syrup into the filling before pouring into the cake pan.

orange, honey & ricotta cheesecake
Prepare the basic recipe, using the finely grated zest of 1 orange instead of the lemon zest.

golden raisin, honey & ricotta cheesecake
Prepare the basic recipe, folding a scant 1/2 cup golden raisins into the filling before baking.

vanilla, honey & ricotta cheesecake
Prepare the basic recipe, replacing the lemon zest with 1 1/2 teaspoons vanilla extract.

cherry, honey & ricotta cheesecake
Prepare the basic recipe, folding a scant 1/2 cup dried cherries into the filling before baking.

variations

creamy lime & blueberry cheesecake

see base recipe page 143

creamy vanilla & blueberry cheesecake
Prepare the basic recipe, omitting the lime zest and juice and adding 1 1/2
teaspoons vanilla extract.

creamy lemon & blueberry cheesecake
Prepare the basic recipe, omitting the lime zest and juice and adding the
finely grated zest and juice of 1 lemon.

creamy orange & blueberry cheesecake
Prepare the basic recipe, omitting the lime zest and juice and adding the
finely grated zest of 1 orange.

creamy vanilla cheesecake
Prepare the basic recipe, omitting the lime zest and juice and the blueberries.
Add 2 teaspoons vanilla extract. Decorate the chilled cheesecake with white
chocolate curls (page 27).

creamy lime cheesecake
Prepare the basic recipe, omitting the blueberries. Add the finely grated
zest and juice of an additional lime. Decorate the chilled cheesecake with
chopped pistachio nuts.

white chocolate cheesecake

see base recipe page 144

raspberry & white chocolate cheesecake
Prepare the basic recipe, omitting the dusting of cocoa powder. Top the
cheesecake with fresh raspberries instead.

strawberry & white chocolate cheesecake
Prepare the basic recipe, omitting the cocoa powder. Top the cheesecake
with fresh strawberries instead.

white & dark chocolate cheesecake
Prepare the basic recipe, decorating the top of the cheesecake with dark
chocolate curls (page 27) before serving.

pure white chocolate cheesecake
Prepare the basic recipe, omitting the dark chocolate chips from the base
and the dusting of cocoa powder. Decorate the top of the cheesecake with
white chocolate curls (page 27).

orange & white chocolate cheesecake
Prepare the basic recipe, omitting the vanilla extract. Add the finely grated
zest of 1 orange to the mixture before baking.

variations

cappuccino cheesecake

see base recipe page 147

coffee & vanilla cheesecake
Prepare the basic recipe, adding 1 teaspoon vanilla extract with the coffee.

coffee & hazelnut cheesecake
Prepare the basic recipe, adding 3 tablespoons finely chopped toasted hazelnuts to the graham cracker crumbs.

coffee toffee cheesecake
Prepare the basic recipe. Serve with dulce de leche drizzled over the top.

coffee & chocolate cheesecake
Prepare the basic recipe, adding 1/4 cup semisweet chocolate chips to the graham cracker crumbs.

coffee & ginger cheesecake
Prepare the basic recipe, using gingersnap crumbs instead of graham cracker crumbs.

variations

black currant cheesecake

see base recipe page 148

orange & black currant cheesecake
Prepare the basic recipe, adding the finely grated zest of 1 orange with the vanilla.

lemon, ginger & black currant cheesecake
Prepare the basic recipe, using gingersnap crumbs instead of graham crackers. Add the finely grated zest of 1 lemon with the vanilla.

summer berry cheesecake
Prepare the basic recipe, substituting a mixture of fresh berries for the black currants. Omit half the water and sugar. When the fruit has simmered, check the flavor and add more sugar if necessary.

blueberry compote cheesecake
Prepare the basic recipe, substituting blueberries for the black currants. Omit half the sugar and water. When the fruit has simmered, check the flavor. Add more sugar if necessary and a squeeze of lemon juice to taste.

cherry compote cheesecake
Prepare the basic recipe, substituting pitted fresh cherries for the black currants. Omit half the sugar and water. When the fruit has simmered, check the sweetness and add a squeeze of lemon juice to taste.

variations

zesty lemon cheesecake

see base recipe page 151

tangy orange cheesecake
Prepare the basic recipe, substituting the finely grated zest of 2 oranges for the lemon zest.

lemon & ginger cheesecake
Prepare the basic recipe, adding 3 chopped pieces of stem ginger in syrup to the filling along with the lemon juice and zest.

zesty lime cheesecake
Prepare the basic recipe, replacing the lemon zest and juice with the finely grated zest of 3 limes and juice of 2 limes.

lemon & hazelnut cheesecake
Prepare the basic recipe, replacing the gingersnaps with 1 1/2 cups graham cracker crumbs and 1/2 cup ground roasted hazelnuts.

lemon & almond cheesecake
Prepare the basic recipe, replacing the gingersnaps with 1 1/2 cups graham cracker crumbs and 1/2 cup ground almonds.

strawberry vanilla cheesecake

see base recipe page 152

raspberry orange cheesecake
Prepare the basic recipe, replacing the vanilla extract with the finely grated zest of 1 orange. Replace the strawberries with raspberries.

very berry cheesecake
Prepare the basic recipe, substituting a mixture of fresh berries for the strawberries.

cherry vanilla cheesecake
Prepare the basic recipe, replacing the strawberries with canned or fresh pitted cherries.

blueberry vanilla cheesecake
Prepare the basic recipe, replacing the strawberries with fresh blueberries.

peach vanilla cheesecake
Prepare the basic recipe, replacing the strawberries with peeled, pitted peaches.

variations

dark chocolate cheesecake

see base recipe page 155

chocolate orange cheesecake
Prepare the basic recipe, adding the finely grated zest of 1 orange with the chocolate.

mocha cheesecake
Prepare the basic recipe, adding 1 tablespoon instant coffee that has been dissolved in 1 tablespoon boiling water to the chocolate-cream cheese mixture.

chocolate raisin cheesecake
Prepare the basic recipe, adding 1/2 cup raisins with the melted chocolate.

chocolate rum cheesecake
Prepare the basic recipe, adding 1 tablespoon rum to the chocolate-cream cheese mixture.

chocolate ginger cheesecake
Prepare the basic recipe, using gingersnap crumbs instead of the graham cracker crumbs.

variations

amaretto cheesecake

see base recipe page 156

amaretto & kahlúa cheesecake
Prepare the basic recipe, using an equal quantity of Kahlúa with the
Amaretto.

amaretto & vanilla cheesecake
Prepare the basic recipe, adding 1 1/2 teaspoons vanilla extract with the
Amaretto.

amaretto & dark chocolate cheesecake
Prepare the basic recipe, stirring 3/4 cup bittersweet chocolate chips into the
cheesecake mixture with the crushed amaretti.

coffee & amaretto cheesecake
Prepare the basic recipe. Dissolve 2 tablespoons instant coffee in
2 tablespoons boiling water, and add it to the filling with the Amaretto.

amaretto & lemon cheesecake
Prepare the basic recipe, stirring the finely grated zest of 1 lemon into the
filling with the Amaretto.

variations

mango cheesecake

see base recipe page 159

mango & passion fruit cheesecake
Prepare the basic recipe, spooning the flesh of 4 or 5 passion fruit over the top of the cheesecake just before serving.

orange, mango & passion fruit cheesecake
Prepare the basic recipe, adding the finely grated zest of 1 orange with the lime juice. Spoon the flesh of 4 or 5 passion fruit over the top of the cheesecake just before serving.

zesty mango cheesecake
Prepare the basic recipe, adding the finely grated zest of 2 limes with the lime juice.

mango & papaya cheesecake
Prepare the basic recipe, topping the cheesecake with slices of 1 to 2 fresh papaya just before serving.

mango & banana cheesecake
Prepare the basic recipe, topping the cheesecake with slices of banana just before serving.

variations

rum raisin cheesecake

see base recipe page 160

cherry kirsch cheesecake
Prepare the basic recipe, using dried cherries instead of the raisins, and kirsch instead of the rum.

rum blueberry cheesecake
Prepare the basic recipe, using dried blueberries instead of the raisins.

vanilla raisin cheesecake
Prepare the basic recipe, omitting the rum and soaking time.

apricot amaretto cheesecake
Prepare the basic recipe, using chopped dried apricots instead of the raisins, and Amaretto instead of the rum.

orange rum raisin cheescake
Prepare the basic recipe, substituting the finely grated zest of 1 orange for the vanilla.

tortes &
gateaux

Rich and elegant tortes, glorious and gorgeous
gateaux — serve them to dinner guests and your
reputation will be golden. But why wait for a party?
These recipes are just as good served with afternoon
tea or morning coffee.

black forest gateau

see variations page 198

This German layer cake is an absolute classic and makes a fabulous dessert cake for a party.

1 3/4 sticks butter, at room
    temperature
3/4 cup superfine sugar
3 eggs
1 2/3 cups self-rising flour
3/4 cup unsweetened cocoa

1/2 cup buttermilk (or 1/4 cup
    milk mixed with 4 tbsp.
    plain yogurt)
1/3 cup milk
two 15-oz. cans pitted cherries,
    drained

4 tbsp. kirsch
2 1/2 cups whipping cream,
    whipped
bittersweet chocolate curls
    (page 27), to decorate

Preheat the oven to 350°F (180°C). Grease a 9-in. (23-cm.) round cake pan, then line the bottom with waxed paper. Beat the butter and sugar until pale and creamy, then beat in the eggs one at a time. Sift the flour and cocoa over the bowl, then fold in. Stir in the buttermilk and milk. Spoon the mixture into the prepared pan and bake for about 45 minutes until risen, and a skewer inserted in the center comes out clean. Let cake cool in the pan for about 15 minutes, then transfer to a wire rack to cool completely. Pick out a few of the best-looking cherries to decorate the top of the cake and set aside. Using a serrated knife, carefully slice the cake horizontally into three layers. Place the bottom layer on a serving plate; drizzle about one-third of the kirsch over it and top with about half the remaining cherries. Spread with about one-quarter of the whipped cream and place the second layer of cake on top. Repeat with more kirsch, cherries, and whipped cream. Top with the remaining cake layer. Drizzle the remaining kirsch over the top layer, then spread whipped cream over the top and sides of the cake. Chill for about 2 hours, then serve decorated with the reserved cherries and dark chocolate curls.

Serves 8–10

sachertorte

see variations page 199

The famous Franz Sacher created this classic torte in Vienna in 1832. Traditionally, the word "Sacher" is piped on top of the chocolate-coated cake.

for the cake
generous 2/3 cup all-purpose flour
4 tbsp. unsweetened cocoa powder
1 stick butter
generous 1 cup superfine sugar
4 eggs, separated

to decorate
2 tbsp. apricot jelly
7 oz. bittersweet chocolate, chopped
3/4 cup whipping cream

Preheat the oven to 350°F (180°C). Grease an 8-in. (20-cm.) round cake pan, then line the bottom with waxed paper. Sift the flour and cocoa together into a large bowl.

In a pan, heat the butter gently until melted, then remove from the heat. Stir in the sugar until well mixed. Beat in the egg yolks. Pour this mixture into the flour–cocoa mixture and stir until just combined.

In a clean bowl, whisk the egg whites until they form soft peaks, then fold into the chocolate mixture, one-third at a time. Tip batter into the prepared cake pan, smoothing out the surface. Bake for about 40 minutes until a skewer inserted in the center comes out clean. Let cool in the pan for about 10 minutes, then turn out onto a wire rack to cool completely. To decorate, warm the jelly slightly to melt, then brush all over the cake. Put the chocolate and cream in a heatproof bowl set over a pan of simmering water and warm, stirring occasionally, until the chocolate has melted. Reserve about 2 tbsp. of the mixture, then pour the rest

over the top and sides of the cake to coat it in a glossy, smooth finish. Spoon the reserved mixture into a piping bag and pipe "Sacher" on the top.

Serves 8

chocolate gateau

see variations page 200

This chocolate gateau is rich and creamy with the refreshing bite of fresh fruit.

for the cake
9 oz. bittersweet chocolate
1 1/2 sticks butter, diced
1 cup superfine sugar
3 extra-large eggs
generous 2/3 cup all-purpose flour
2 tbsp. instant coffee dissolved in 2 tbsp.
   boiling water

for the frosting
2 cups unsweetened chocolate, chopped
2/3 stick unsalted butter
to decorate
2 cups mixed berries

Preheat the oven to 325°F (160°C). Grease an 8-in. (20-cm.) springform pan and line the bottom with waxed paper. Break the chocolate into pieces and put in a heatproof bowl with the butter. Place the bowl over a pan of gently simmering water and heat gently until the chocolate and butter have melted. Remove from the heat and let cool. Stir in the sugar, then beat in the eggs, one at a time. Sift the flour over the mixture, then fold in. Stir in the coffee. Tip the mixture into the prepared pan and bake for 55 minutes until firm on top, with a slight wobble in the center. (The cake will firm as it cools.) Let cool in the pan.

Carefully unmold the cake onto a cutting board and divide into two layers (page 21). Melt the chocolate with the butter over a double boiler or simmering pan of water, stirring to combine. Remove from the heat once melted and thickened, and let cool. Place the cake on a serving dish and spread 1/3 mixture on top of one layer. Sandwich with the other, and smooth the top and sides of the cake with chocolate frosting. Decorate with berries.

Serves 8

boston cream pie

see variations page 201

Don't be fooled by the name of this wonderful confection. It's actually a cake, layered with thick vanilla custard and topped with a melting chocolate ganache.

for the cake
1 1/2 sticks butter, at room
    temperature
3/4 cup superfine sugar
3 eggs
scant 1 1/4 cups self-rising
    flour

1 tsp. vanilla extract
for the custard
1/2 cup milk
3/4 cup light cream
3 egg yolks
2 tbsp. superfine sugar

2 tbsp. all-purpose flour
1 tsp. vanilla extract
for the chocolate ganache
3 1/2 oz. bittersweet chocolate
scant 1/2 cup whipping cream

Preheat oven to 350°F (180°C). Grease two 8-in. (20-cm.) round cake pans, then line the bottoms with waxed paper.

Beat together the butter and sugar until pale and fluffy. Beat in the eggs one at a time. Sift the flour over the bowl, add the vanilla extract, and stir until thoroughly combined. Spoon the batter into the cake pans and spread out evenly using the back of the spoon. Bake for 20 to 25 minutes until golden brown and the cake springs back when pressed lightly with your fingertips. Turn the cakes out onto a wire rack, gently peel off the waxed paper, and let cool completely. Meanwhile, make the custard. Warm the milk and cream in a pan until almost boiling, then set aside. In a bowl, whisk together the egg yolks and sugar until creamy, add the vanilla extract, then whisk in the flour. Whisking constantly, slowly pour in the hot milk, then pour back into the pan. Heat gently, stirring, for about 2 minutes until thick.

Pour into a bowl, press plastic wrap over the surface, cool, then chill. To serve, spread the chilled custard over one of the cakes, then place the second cake on top.

Chop the chocolate finely and put in a heatproof bowl. Heat the cream until almost boiling, then pour it over the chocolate and let stand for 5 minutes. Stir until smooth. Allow to cool and thicken slightly, then pour over the cake.

Serves 8

chocolate & ginger torte

see variations page 202

Light and crumbly on the outside and moist and melting on the inside, this divine chocolate torte is perfect served for dessert with thick cream poured over the top.

5 oz. semisweet chocolate, chopped
3/4 stick butter
3 extra-large eggs, separated
1/3 cup all-purpose flour

3 pieces of stem ginger in syrup, chopped
generous 1/4 cup superfine sugar
unsweetened cocoa powder, to dust
heavy cream, to serve

Preheat oven to 325°F (160°C). Grease an 8-in. (20-cm.) round springform cake pan and line its base with waxed paper.

Put the chocolate and butter in a heatproof bowl set over a pan of barely simmering water. Heat until melted. Remove from the heat and cool for about 10 minutes. Beat in the egg yolks, then sift the flour over the top and fold in, along with the chopped ginger.

In a separate bowl, whisk the egg whites until foamy, then whisk in the sugar, 1 tbsp. at a time, until peaks are formed. Fold egg whites into the chocolate mixture, then pour into the prepared cake pan. Bake for about 25 minutes until firm to the touch, but still slightly soft in the center. Let cool completely in the pan.

To serve, remove the cake from the pan, and dust with cocoa powder. Serve in wedges with heavy cream poured on top.

Serves 8

coffee & praline layer cake

see variations page 203

Praline is incredibly simple to make, and is a stunning topping for this luscious, creamy layer cake. Decorate the cake with praline just before serving.

for the cake
1 1/2 sticks butter, at room temperature
generous 3/4 cup superfine sugar
3 eggs
scant 1 1/4 cups self-rising flour
2 1/2 tsp. instant coffee, dissolved in
    1 tbsp. hot water
1/2 cup toasted hazelnuts, roughly chopped

for the praline
1/4 cup superfine sugar
1/3 cup toasted hazelnuts
for the frosting
7 oz. mascarpone
1 3/4 cups confectioners' sugar, sifted
1 tbsp. instant coffee, dissolved in 1 tbsp.
    boiling water

Preheat oven to 350°F (180°C). Grease two 8-in. (20-cm.) round cake pans, then line the bottoms with waxed paper.

Beat the butter and sugar together until pale and creamy, then beat in the eggs one at a time. Sift the flour over the butter mixture and stir in. Fold in the nuts and coffee, then divide the batter between the two pans and spread out evenly. Bake for 20 to 25 minutes until golden, and the cake springs back when pressed gently. Transfer to a wire rack to cool. To make the praline, line a baking sheet with waxed paper. Put the sugar in a heavy pan and heat gently, stirring, for about 5 minutes until melted and pale golden. Add the hazelnuts and stir for about 30 seconds, then pour onto the baking sheet and let harden for 20 minutes. To make the frosting, beat together the mascarpone, sugar, and coffee until smooth and creamy. Spread slightly less than half the frosting over one of the cooled cakes,

then place the second cake on top. Swirl the remaining frosting on top. Break the praline into shards and use it to decorate the cake.

Serves 8

strawberry hazelnut gateau

see variations page 204

This simple, light, creamy gateau is perfect to serve for dessert, or for a summer afternoon tea when strawberries are in season and at their sweet and juicy best.

for the cake
2/3 cup toasted hazelnuts
1 1/2 sticks butter, at room
temperature
3/4 cup superfine sugar

3 eggs
1 cup self-rising flour
to decorate
1 cup whipping cream

1 cup strawberries, hulled and
roughly chopped, plus extra
to decorate
1 cup toasted hazelnuts,
roughly chopped

Preheat the oven to 350°F (180°C). Grease two 8-in. (20-cm.) round cake pans, then line the bases with waxed paper.

Put hazelnuts in a food processor and process until finely ground. Beat together the butter and sugar until pale and fluffy. Beat in the eggs one at a time. Sift the flour over the top, add the ground hazelnuts, and fold in until combined. Spoon the mixture into prepared pans and spread out evenly using the back of the spoon. Bake for 20 to 25 minutes until golden brown and the cakes spring back when pressed lightly. Turn the cakes out onto a wire rack, gently peel off the waxed paper, and let cool completely. Just before serving, whip the cream until it stands in soft peaks. Spoon slightly less than half the whipped cream into a bowl. Fold in the chopped strawberries and half the chopped hazelnuts. Spoon the mixture on top of one cake and top with the second cake. Swirl the remaining cream on top, sprinkle with the remaining hazelnuts, and decorate with more strawberries.

Serves 8

banoffee gateau

see variations page 205

Inspired by the classic banana and toffee pie, this luxurious and indulgent cake makes a great dessert or a wicked treat for afternoon tea.

for the cake
1 1/2 sticks butter, at room temperature
3/4 cup superfine sugar
3 eggs
scant 1 1/4 cups self-rising flour
1 tsp. vanilla extract

for the filling
1 cup whipping cream
2 medium-large bananas, sliced
5 tbsp. dulce de leche
grated bittersweet chocolate, for sprinkling

Preheat the oven to 350°F (180°C). Grease two 8-in. (20-cm.) round cake pans, then line the bottoms with waxed paper.

Beat together the butter and sugar until pale and fluffy. Beat in the eggs one at a time. Sift the flour over the bowl and stir in until thoroughly combined. Fold in the vanilla.

Spoon the cake batter into the prepared pans and spread out evenly using the back of the spoon. Bake for 20 to 25 minutes until golden brown and the cake springs back when pressed lightly with the tips of your fingers. Turn the cakes out onto a wire rack, gently peel off the waxed paper, and let cool completely.

To serve, whip the cream, then spread about half over one of the cakes. Drizzle about 2 1/2 tbsp. dulce de leche over the cake and top with about half the banana slices.

Place the second cake on top, swirl with the remaining whipped cream, drizzle with the remaining dulce de leche, and top with the remaining banana slices. Decorate with a sprinkle of grated chocolate and serve immediately.

Serves 8

apricot almond torte

see variations page 206

Moist and buttery with the unmistakable sharp tang of apricots, this torte makes a wonderful dessert cake served either warm or cold with a generous dollop or two of crème fraîche.

1 1/2 sticks butter, at room temperature
3/4 cup superfine sugar
2 extra-large eggs
1 1/4 cups ground almonds
2/3 cup all-purpose flour
1 1/2 tsp. baking powder

1 tsp. ground cinnamon
about 3/4 lb. fresh apricots, unpeeled, halved, and pitted
confectioners' sugar, for dusting
crème fraîche, to serve

Preheat the oven to 350°F (180°C). Grease a 9-in (20-cm.) round springform cake pan, and line the bottom with waxed paper. Beat together the butter and sugar until smooth and creamy, then beat in the eggs. Stir in the ground almonds. Combine the flour, baking powder, and cinnamon. Sift over the egg mixture, then fold in.

Spoon the mixture into the prepared pan, spreading it out evenly, then arrange the apricots on top. Bake for about 45 minutes until golden, then cover with a sheet of foil. Bake for another 20 minutes until a skewer inserted into the center of the cake comes out clean.

Let the cake cool in the pan for about 10 minutes, then transfer to a wire rack to cool. Serve warm or cold, dusted with confectioners' sugar and large dollops of crème fraîche.

Serves 8

creamy apple torte

see variations page 207

Sharp and sweet, this almost mousselike cake has a really tangy flavor that contrasts deliciously with the vanilla cream filling.

for the cake
3/4 stick butter
2 large cooking apples (about
    1 1/2 lbs.), peeled, cored,
    and sliced
generous 1/3 cup crème fraîche

finely grated zest and juice of
    3/4 lemon
3/4 cup superfine sugar
1 1/2 tbsp. all-purpose flour
6 eggs, separated
5 tbsp. slivered almonds
confectioners' sugar, to dust

for the filling
1 1/3 cups crème fraîche
1/2 tsp. vanilla extract
4 tsp. confectioners' sugar,
    sifted

Preheat oven to 325°F (160°C). Grease three 8-in. (20-cm.) springform round cake pans, then line the bottoms with waxed paper.

Melt the butter in a pan and gently fry the apples for about 8 minutes, stirring frequently, until tender and pulpy. Beat together the crème fraîche, lemon zest and juice, sugar, flour, and egg yolks. Stir into the apples. Continue cooking gently, stirring, for about 5 minutes, until thickened. Pour into a clean bowl and set aside to cool.

In a clean bowl, whisk the egg whites until they form stiff peaks. Stir the cooled apple mixture, then fold in a couple of spoonfuls of egg whites to loosen. Fold in the remaining egg whites, one-third at a time. Divide the mixture among the lined pans and spread out evenly. Scatter the almonds over the cakes, then bake for about 45 minutes until firm and golden.

Let cool in the pans. Run a knife around the inside of each cake pan, then carefully turn each cake onto a flat plate. Gently peel off the lining paper, then place another plate over the top and flip over so the cake sits the right way up. Cover with plastic wrap and chill.

To make the filling, combine the crème fraîche, vanilla, and sugar. Spread half the cream mixture on top of one of the cakes and cover with another cake. Spread it with the remaining cream. Carefully place the final cake on top, and dust with confectioners' sugar. Serve cold.

Serves 8

tropical fruit gateau

see variations page 208

With a delicate coconut sponge cake, creamy filling, and mounds of tropical fruit, this fabulous cake will bring a taste of sunshine into your home.

for the cake
1 stick plus 1 tbsp. butter, at room temperature
3 tbsp. creamed coconut, at room temperature
3/4 cup superfine sugar
3 eggs
1 cup self-rising flour
scant 2/3 cup shredded coconut

for the filling
1 cup whipping cream
1/2 large mango, pitted, peeled, and sliced
1 medium-large banana, peeled and sliced
one 8-oz. can pineapple chunks
fresh coconut shavings

Preheat the oven to 350°F (180°C). Grease two 8-in. (20-cm.) round cake pans and line the bottoms with waxed paper.

Beat together the butter, creamed coconut, and sugar until pale and creamy. Beat in the eggs, one at a time. Sift the flour over the bowl, then fold in. Stir in the shredded coconut. Spoon the batter into the prepared pans and spread out evenly using the back of the spoon. Bake for 20 to 25 minutes until golden brown and a skewer inserted in the center comes out clean. Turn the cakes out onto a wire rack and let cool completely.

Just before serving, whip the cream. Spread about half over one of the cakes. Top with about half the banana, pineapple, and mango. Place the second cake on top. Swirl the remaining whipped cream on top and pile on the remaining fruit. Garnish with coconut shavings.

Serves 8

raspberry & white chocolate torte

see variations page 209

This light, fluffy white chocolate cake relies on whisked egg whites to help it rise and give it its melt-in-the-mouth texture. Sharp, tangy raspberries offset the vanilla sweetness of the cake wonderfully.

5 oz. white chocolate
1 stick plus 1/2 tbsp butter
2/3 cup superfine sugar
4 extra-large eggs, separated
1 tsp. vanilla extract

2/3 cup all-purpose flour
1/4 cup ground almonds
1 1/3 cups fresh raspberries
confectioners' sugar, to dust
whipping cream, to serve

Preheat oven to 325°F (160°C). Grease a 9-in. (23-cm.) springform pan and line its base with waxed paper.

Break the chocolate into a heatproof bowl set over a pan of barely simmering water. Heat until melted. Remove from the heat and let cool for about 10 minutes.

Beat together the butter and half the sugar until smooth and creamy, then beat in the egg yolks one at a time. Stir in the vanilla and melted chocolate. Sift the flour over the bowl and add the almonds. Fold together gently.

In a separate bowl, whisk the egg whites until foamy, then whisk in the remaining sugar 1 tbsp. at time until thick and glossy and peaks have formed. Fold a small amount at a time into the chocolate mixture. Pour the batter into the prepared pan and bake for 35 to 40 minutes until risen and golden and a skewer inserted into the center comes out clean.

Let the cake cool in the pan for about 10 minutes, then remove the ring and let the cake cool on the base. To serve, top with fresh raspberries, dust with confectioners' sugar, and offer with a pitcher of cream.

Serves 8–10

variations

black forest gateau

see base recipe page 175

strawberry-chocolate gateau
Use 3 1/2 cups sliced strawberries instead of cherries.

raspberry-chocolate gateau
Use 2 2/3 cups fresh raspberries instead of the cherries and decorate with white chocolate instead of bittersweet chocolate curls.

fig & walnut chocolate gateau
Prepare the basic recipe, adding 1/2 cup chopped walnuts to the cake batter. Decorate the finished cake with quartered fresh figs and walnut halves. Omit the chocolate curls.

orange chocolate gateau
Omit the cherries from the basic recipe. Cut away the peel and white pith from 2 oranges, then slice between the membranes to remove the segments of flesh. Assemble the cake using the orange segments instead of the cherries.

nutty black forest gateau
Prepare the basic recipe, adding 1/2 cup chopped toasted hazelnuts to the cake batter. Sprinkle the finished cake with more chopped toasted hazelnuts to decorate.

sachertorte

see base recipe page 176

strawberry sachertorte
Omit the apricot jelly. Instead, carefully slice the cooled cake horizontally, then sandwich the two layers with about 4 tablespoons strawberry jelly. Warm another 2 tablespoons strawberry jelly in a pan, and brush over the cake before icing.

cherry sachertorte
Substitute 2 tablespoons strained cherry jelly for the apricot jelly. Decorate the frosted cake with whipped cream and canned pitted cherries.

orange sachertorte
Prepare the basic recipe, adding the finely grated zest of 1 orange with the egg yolks. Substitute 2 tablespoons strained marmalade for the apricot jelly.

mocha sachertorte
Add 2 tablespoons instant coffee dissolved in 2 tablespoons boiling water with the egg yolks. Add 1 tablespoon instant coffee to the saucepan with the cream and chocolate to make the topping.

cinnamon sachertorte
Add 1 1/2 teaspoons ground cinnamon to the cocoa powder and flour.

variations

chocolate gateau

see base recipe page 178

white & dark chocolate gateau
Substitute the unsweetened chocolate in the frosting with white chocolate.
Decorate with bittersweet chocolate curls, omitting the berries.

mandarin chocolate gateau
Add the zest of 1 orange to the cake mix. Decorate with mandarin slices
rather than berries.

strawberry chocolate gateau
Use 1 teaspoon vanilla extract instead of coffee in the cake. Use sliced fresh
strawberries to decorate, instead of the mixed berries.

coffee mascarpone gateau
Prepare the basic recipe. Substitute the chocolate frosting for 1 tablespoon
instant coffee dissolved in 1 tablespoon boiling water, cooled and mixed with
2 cups mascarpone cheese. Omit the fruit. Dust with unsweetened cocoa.

chocolate & walnut gateau
Prepare the basic recipe, adding 1 cup chopped walnuts to the cake mix.
Omit the fruit, and decorate with walnut halves.

variations

boston cream pie

see base recipe page 180

coffee cream pie
Add 1 tablespoon instant coffee dissolved in 1 tablespoon boiling water to
the cake batter. Add 1 tablespoon instant coffee dissolved in 1 tablespoon
boiling water to the milk and cream before warming.

double chocolate cream pie
Add 2 tablespoons unsweetened cocoa powder to the cake batter with the
flour. To make the custard, stir 1 to 2 tablespoons milk into 1 tablespoon
unsweetened cocoa powder to make a paste, then stir into the rest of the
milk before heating with the cream.

raspberry cream pie
Omit the chocolate ganache. Top the custard with 1 cup fresh raspberries.
Cover with the second cake and dust with confectioners' sugar.

hazelnut cream pie
Stir 1 cup chopped toasted hazelnuts into the cake batter.

blueberry cream pie
Omit the chocolate ganache. Top the custard with 1 cup blueberries, before
covering with the second cake and dusting with confectioners' sugar.

variations

chocolate & ginger torte

see base recipe page 183

plain chocolate torte
Prepare the basic recipe, omitting the stem ginger.

raspberry chocolate torte
Prepare the basic recipe, omitting the stem ginger, and topping the cooled cake with about 1 1/3 cups fresh raspberries.

chocolate orange torte
Prepare the basic recipe, using the finely grated zest of 2 oranges instead of the stem ginger.

mocha torte
Prepare the basic recipe, omitting the stem ginger. Dissolve 2 tablespoons instant coffee in 1 1/2 tablespoons boiling water and add to the cake batter.

strawberry chocolate torte
Prepare the basic recipe, omitting the stem ginger. Serve with fresh hulled strawberries on the side.

coffee & praline layer cake

see base recipe page 184

coffee & peanut brittle cake
Prepare the basic recipe, using unsalted peanuts instead of the hazelnuts.

coffee & pecan brittle cake
Prepare the basic recipe, using pecans instead of the hazelnuts.

chocolate-coffee praline cake
Prepare the basic recipe, stirring 2 tablespoons unsweetened cocoa powder into the cake batter with the flour.

coffee toffee cake
Prepare the basic recipe, drizzling the filling with 2 tablespoons dulce de leche before covering with the second cake, then drizzling more dulce de leche on top.

coffee, praline & chocolate chip cake
Prepare the basic recipe, sprinkling the filling with 1/8 cup bittersweet chocolate chips and the top of the cake with another 1/8 cup.

variations

strawberry hazelnut gateau

see base recipe page 187

raspberry hazelnut gateau
Substitute whole fresh raspberries for the strawberries.

lemon, strawberry & hazelnut gateau
Prepare the basic recipe, adding the finely grated zest of 1 lemon to the cake batter with the flour and nuts.

mango almond gateau
Prepare the basic recipe, omitting the hazelnuts and strawberries. Substitute toasted almonds for the hazelnuts and chopped mangoes for the chopped strawberries. Decorate the cake with mango slices instead of the whole strawberries.

banana hazelnut gateau
Prepare the basic recipe, using chopped banana instead of the chopped strawberries. Use sliced banana to decorate the cake.

strawberry, hazelnut & white chocolate gateau
Prepare the basic recipe, decorating the finished cake with strawberries and white chocolate curls (page 27) and omitting the final sprinkling of chopped hazelnuts.

variations

banoffee gateau

see base recipe page 188

chocolate banoffee gateau
Add 2 tablespoons cocoa powder with the flour.

ginger banoffee gateau
Omit the vanilla extract. Instead, fold 1 teaspoon ground ginger and
3 chopped pieces of stem ginger in syrup into the cake batter. Fold
2 additional pieces of chopped stem ginger in syrup into the whipped
cream before spreading over the cake.

coffee toffee gateau
Omit the vanilla extract and the bananas. Dissolve 1 tablespoon instant coffee
in 1 tablespoon boiling water and fold into the cake batter just before baking.

chocolate chip banoffee gateau
Sprinkle 2 tablespoons chocolate chips over the whipped cream between the
layers, and another 2 tablespoons chocolate chips over the top of the cake.

hazelnut banoffee gateau
Fold 1/2 cup chopped toasted hazelnuts into the cake batter. Sprinkle 1/2 cup
chopped toasted hazelnuts over the whipped cream between the layers, and
an additional 1/2 cup chopped toasted hazelnuts over the top of the cake.

variations

apricot almond torte

see base recipe page 191

plum almond torte
Prepare the basic recipe, replacing the apricots with plums.

vanilla apricot torte
Prepare the basic recipe, using 1 teaspoon vanilla extract instead of ground cinnamon.

cinnamon almond torte
Prepare the basic recipe, omitting the apricots.

raspberry almond torte
Prepare the basic recipe, omitting the apricots. Serve topped with about 1 2/3 cups fresh raspberries.

strawberry almond torte
Prepare the basic recipe, omitting the apricots. Serve topped with about 2 cups fresh sliced or halved strawberries.

variations

creamy apple torte

see base recipe page 192

creamy cinnamon apple torte
Prepare the basic recipe, adding 1 teaspoon ground cinnamon to the
cooked apples.

creamy apple torte with lemon cream filling
Prepare the basic recipe, omitting the vanilla and confectioners' sugar
in the filling, and instead combining 3 tablespoons lemon curd with the
crème fraîche.

creamy apple & hazelnut torte
Prepare the basic recipe, substituting roughly chopped toasted hazelnuts for
the slivered almonds.

creamy apple & walnut torte
Prepare the basic recipe, substituting roughly chopped walnuts for the
slivered almonds.

creamy apple & blueberry torte
Prepare the basic recipe, sprinkling about 2 2/3 cups fresh blueberries over
the filling between the layers.

variations

tropical fruit gateau

see base recipe page 195

coconut & mango gateau
Prepare the basic recipe, using 1 pitted, peeled, sliced mango and omitting the banana and pineapple.

coconut & papaya gateau
Prepare the basic recipe, using 2 seeded, peeled, and sliced papayas in place of the mixed tropical fruits, squeezing a little lime juice over the papaya. Omit the mango, banana, and pineapple.

coconut & banana gateau
Prepare the basic recipe, using 2 or 3 peeled, sliced bananas and omitting the mango and pineapple.

coconut & pineapple gateau
Prepare the basic recipe, using 2 cans of pineapple chunks and omitting the mango and banana.

raspberry & white chocolate torte

see base recipe page 196

blueberry & white chocolate torte
Spread the cooled cake with whipped cream and top with fresh blueberries instead of raspberries.

peach melba torte
Use sliced peaches instead of raspberries. Put 2 cups of fresh raspberries in a blender and purée. Strain through a sieve to remove the seeds, then sweeten with about 1/2 tablespoon confectioners' sugar, to taste. Serve the torte with the raspberry sauce spooned on top.

mango & white chocolate torte
Use slices of fresh mango instead of raspberries.

strawberry & white chocolate torte
Omit the raspberries and dust the torte with confectioners' sugar instead. Blend 3 cups of fresh strawberries, then press them through a sieve to remove the seeds. Serve the torte with the strawberry sauce spooned on top.

simple white chocolate torte
Prepare the basic recipe, omitting the raspberries and confectioners' sugar. Simply dust the torte with unsweetened cocoa powder before serving.

special occasion cakes

What could be a better way to mark a special

occasion than by baking a really magnificent cake?

These recipes are easy too, leaving you relaxed,

refreshed, and ready to party when your cake

makes its big entrance.

white wedding cake

see variations page 234

This is the easiest and prettiest white wedding cake you can make — a simple lemon cake frosted with buttercream and decorated with fresh rose petals.

for the cake
2 1/4 sticks butter, at room
    temperature
1 1/3 cups superfine sugar
finely grated zest of 2 small
    lemons

4 eggs
1 2/3 cups self-rising flour
for the frosting
2 1/4 sticks butter, at room
    temperature

3 2/3 cups confectioners'
    sugar, sifted
4 tbsp. milk
1/2 tsp. vanilla extract
white or cream rose petals, to
    decorate

To make a tiered wedding cake, make the small and large wedding cakes (page 234) as well, then use cake pillars to stack them together.

Preheat oven to 350°F (180°C). Grease two 8-in. (20-cm.) round cake pans and line the bottoms with waxed paper. Beat the butter and sugar until pale and creamy, then add the lemon zest. Beat in the eggs one at a time. Sift the flour over the bowl, then fold in. Divide the batter evenly between the two pans and bake for about 30 minutes until risen and golden and a skewer inserted in the center comes out clean. Turn the cakes out on a wire rack to cool completely. For the frosting, beat together the butter, confectioners' sugar, milk, and vanilla until smooth and creamy. Place one of the cakes on a cake board and spread a layer of buttercream frosting over the top. Place the second cake on top and fill in any gaps between the two cakes with more buttercream to create flat sides. Swirl buttercream over the top and sides of the cake. Scatter the top and the cake board with rose petals.

chocolate wedding cake

see variations page 235

If you want something more luscious than the usual white wedding cake, this is the recipe for you — rich, dark, and oozing with chocolate.

for the cake
3 oz. semisweet chocolate
1 1/2 sticks butter, at room temperature
1/4 cup light brown sugar
1/2 cup superfine sugar
3 eggs

scant 1 1/4 cups self-rising flour
3 tbsp. unsweetened cocoa powder
1 tsp. ground cinnamon

to decorate
4 tbsp. raspberry jelly
6 oz. semisweet chocolate
3/4 cup whipping cream
bittersweet chocolate curls (page 27), to decorate
unsweetened cocoa powder, for dusting (optional)

To make a tiered wedding cake, make the small and large wedding cakes (page 235) as well, then use cake pillars to stack them together.

Preheat oven to 350°F (180°C). Grease an 8-in. (20-cm.) springform cake pan and line the bottom with waxed paper. Break the chocolate into a heatproof bowl set over a pan of barely simmering water, and warm until melted. Remove from the heat and set aside to cool. Beat the butter and sugars until pale and creamy, then beat in the eggs one at a time. Sift the flour, cocoa and cinnamon over the top, then fold in, followed by the melted chocolate. Spoon into the prepared pan and bake for about 50 minutes until risen, and a skewer inserted in the center comes out clean. Turn out onto a wire rack to cool completely.

To decorate, slice the cake in half horizontally and spread with the jelly. Place the second cake on top to create a perfect fit with straight sides. Put the chocolate and cream in a

heatproof bowl set over a pan of barely simmering water and warm, stirring occasionally, until the chocolate has melted. Let cool and thicken slightly, then pour over the cake to cover the top and sides completely. Decorate the top of the cake with chocolate curls and dust with cocoa.

spring flower cake

see variations page 236

This light, fresh, lemony layer cake is perfect for celebrating Mother's Day. Alternatively, make it as a gift to take to a spring lunch party or enjoy it with guests.

for the cake
1 1/2 sticks butter, at room temperature
3/4 cup superfine sugar
finely grated zest of 1 lemon
3 eggs
scant 1 1/4 cups self-rising flour

to decorate
9 1/2 oz. cream cheese
generous 1/3 cup confectioners' sugar, sifted
finely grated zest of 1 lemon, plus 2 tsp. juice
3 tbsp. lemon curd
sugared flower petals (page 27), to decorate

Preheat the oven to 350°F (180°C). Grease two 8-in. (20-cm.) round cake pans, and line the bottoms with waxed paper.

Beat together the butter, sugar, and lemon zest until pale and creamy, then beat in the eggs one at a time. Sift the flour over the bowl, then fold in. Divide the batter between the two cake pans, spreading out evenly with the back of a spoon. Bake for 20 to 25 minutes until risen and golden and a skewer inserted in the center comes out clean. Turn out onto a wire rack and let cool completely.

To make the frosting, beat together the cream cheese, confectioners' sugar, lemon zest, and lemon juice until smooth and creamy. Spread lemon curd over one cake, then spread just less than half the cream cheese frosting on top. Cover with the second cake and swirl with the remaining frosting. Decorate with sugared flowers.

Serves 8

halloween cake

see variations page 237

Get scary at Halloween with this fabulously moist and succulent cake made with roast squash or pumpkin. Look for toy spiders in toy shops to decorate the cake and plate with. (Just remember to warn your guests they're not edible — in case they get carried away!)

for the cake
3/4 lb. peeled, seeded
    butternut squash or
    pumpkin, cut into chunks
1/2 tbsp. vegetable oil
1 stick butter, at room
    temperature

3/4 cup light brown sugar
3 eggs
1/2 tsp. ground ginger
1 1/2 tsp. ground cinnamon
scant 1 1/4 cups self-rising
    flour

to decorate
7 oz. bittersweet chocolate,
    chopped
generous 3/4 cup whipping
    cream
1 oz. white chocolate

Preheat oven to 375°F (190°C). Put squash in a baking dish, drizzle with the oil, and toss to coat. Roast for about 35 minutes until tender. Remove and let cool, then mash to a coarse purée.

Preheat oven to 350°F (180°C). Grease an 8-in. (20-cm.) round cake pan and line the bottom with waxed paper. Beat the butter and sugar together until smooth and creamy. Beat in the eggs one at a time, then stir in the ginger and cinnamon. Sift the flour over the bowl and fold in, then fold in the mashed squash.

Fill the cake pan and bake for about 50 minutes until risen and a skewer inserted into the center comes out clean. Transfer to a wire rack to cool completely.

To decorate, put the chopped bittersweet chocolate in a heatproof bowl. Heat the cream until almost boiling, then pour over the chocolate. Let stand for 5 minutes, then stir until smooth. Let cool and thicken slightly.

Melt the white chocolate in a heatproof bowl set over a pan of barely simmering water. Pour the dark chocolate frosting over the cake, then spoon the melted white chocolate into a piping bag. Pipe concentric circles on the cake. Draw a skewer from the center to the outside to create a spider web effect.

Serves 8

sparkling fireworks cake

see variations page 238

This chocolate cake makes a great dessert or centerpiece for any celebration. Serve it as it is, or with cream poured over the top.

for the cake
1 stick butter
4 1/2 oz. bittersweet chocolate
6 eggs, separated
1 tsp. vanilla extract

1/3 cup superfine sugar
1 1/2 cups ground almonds
for the frosting
3 1/2 oz. bittersweet chocolate, chopped

generous 1/3 cup whipping cream
silver dragées and sparklers, to decorate*

Preheat oven to 325°F (170°C). Grease a 9-in. (23-cm.) cake pan and line base with waxed paper. Put butter and chocolate in a heatproof bowl over a pan of barely simmering water. Let it melt, stir until smooth, and set aside to cool for about 10 minutes.

Stir in egg yolks, vanilla, one-third of the sugar, and ground almonds. In a separate bowl, whisk the egg whites until they form soft peaks, then continue whisking, sprinkling the remaining sugar 1 tbsp. at a time over the whites, until stiff peaks form. Fold 2 tablespoonfuls of the whites into the chocolate-almond mixture, then fold in the rest, one-third at a time. Spoon batter into cake pan and bake for about 30 minutes until risen and firm. Let it cool in pan before turning out onto a plate. To make the frosting, put chocolate in a heatproof bowl. Heat cream until almost boiling, then pour it over the chocolate and let stand for about 5 minutes. Stir until smooth, then let cool until thick. Spread frosting over the cake. To serve, sprinkle with tiny silver dragées, stud the cake with mini indoor sparklers, and light.

Serves 8–10

*silver dragées are illegal in some states so only purchase them from reputable stores

loveheart valentine's cake

see variations page 239

Pretty as a picture, this gorgeous heart-shaped cake is surprisingly easy to make and will leave your lover feeling adored!

1 stick plus 1 tbsp. butter, at room temperature
2/3 cup superfine sugar
3 eggs
1 tsp. vanilla extract
scant 1 1/4 cups self-rising flour
1 cup red currants, plus extra to decorate
3-4 tbsp. red currant jelly

3 1/2 oz. mascarpone
2 tbsp. confectioners' sugar, sifted
pink food coloring
pink edible glitter, for sprinkling
rice paper roses, to decorate

Preheat the oven to 350°F (180°C). Grease an 8-in. (20-cm.) springform square cake pan and line the bottom with waxed paper.

Beat the butter and sugar together until pale and creamy, then beat in the eggs one at a time followed by the vanilla. Sift the flour over the mixture and fold in. Add the red currants and fold in gently. Spoon the batter into the cake pan and spread out evenly. Bake for about 30 minutes until risen and golden and a skewer inserted in the center comes out clean. Let cool in the pan for about 5 minutes, then transfer to a wire rack to cool completely.

Meanwhile, cut out an 8-in. (20-cm.) square of paper and draw a heart inside, going right up to the edges. Cut out to make a template. When the cake is completely cooled, place the template on top and use a serrated knife to carefully trim the cake into a heart shape.

Then carefully slice the cake in half using a serrated knife. Sandwich the halves together with the red currant jelly. Beat together the mascarpone and sugar until smooth and creamy, then stir in a little pink food coloring to achieve a pretty pastel pink. Spread the frosting over the cake, dust with pink glitter, and decorate with more red currants and rice paper roses.

Serves 8

ginger & lime ice cream birthday cake

see variations page 240

This is a fabulous no-bake cake that makes an excellent dessert for a special birthday lunch or dinner. For a children's birthday party, try one of the variations such as vanilla or chocolate.

for the cake
2 cups prepared custard
3 1/2 pieces stem ginger in syrup, chopped
finely grated zest and juice of 2 limes

1 cup whipping cream
about 10 oz. store-bought
    gingerbread or ginger cake

Put the custard in a bowl and stir in the ginger, lime zest, and lime juice. Fold in the whipping cream and churn in an ice cream maker until thick and a soft scooping consistency. (If you don't have an ice cream maker, whip cream until thick and standing in soft peaks. Fold into the custard, then freeze in a freezer container. Beat with a fork after 2 hours to break up the ice crystals, then beat every 30 minutes until you achieve the desired consistency.)

Meanwhile, grease an 8-in. (20-cm.) round springform pan and line the bottom with waxed paper. Trim off the outside of the cake, then slice the cake about 3/8-in. (7-mm.) thick. Line the sides of the pan with the slices, then cut pieces to cover the base neatly. Spoon the semifrozen ice cream into the cake-lined pan and freeze for 3 to 4 hours until firm. To serve, decorate the top of the cake with flaming candles, and serve in wedges.

Serves 8

golden christmas cake

see variations page 241

You'll wow your holiday guests with this stunning cake. It's simple to make, but remember to allow at least 24 hours before frosting the cake to allow the marzipan to dry.

7-in. (18-cm.) fruit cake (such as Nut-free Fruit
    Cake, page 90)
to decorate
5 oz. ready-to-roll fondant icing
edible gold powder
10 oz. marzipan

1/2 cup apricot jelly, strained
3 egg whites
4 cups confectioners' sugar
1 tbsp. lemon juice
14 oz. white and gold candy-coated almonds
gold dragées*

Roll out the fondant icing on a piece of plastic wrap. Cut out lots of Christmas shapes using 1 1/2-in. (4-cm.) and 2-in. (5-cm.) cookie cutters. Dust with gold dust, then set aside to harden.

Turn cake upside down onto a cake serving plate. Knead about 2 oz. marzipan until soft, then shape into a sausage and tuck it around the base of the cake to give it straight sides all the way down. Roll out the remaining marzipan to a 14-in. (35-cm.) round.

Warm the jelly in a saucepan until runny, then brush all over the cake. Lay the marzipan circle on top and smooth it over the cake, patting gently to flatten all over. With a knife, trim off any excess. Let dry for at least 24 hours.

To ice the cake, put the egg whites in a bowl and whisk, gradually sifting in the confectioners' sugar until the mixture forms stiff peaks. Beat in the lemon juice, then swirl

*dragées are illegal in some states so only purchase them from reputable stores

the frosting all over the marzipan-covered cake. Set aside for about 2 hours to allow the frosting to firm up.

Arrange about half of the gold shapes, candy-coated almonds, and gold balls on top of the cake, then scatter the remaining shapes, almonds, and balls around the base.

Serves 10

pear & cranberry christmas cake

see variations page 242

This light, fruity cake, which combines the delicate flavor of pear with the sharp tang of cranberries, makes a wonderful alternative to a traditional fruit cake.

1 1/2 sticks butter,
   at room temperature
3/4 cup superfine sugar
3 eggs
1 1/3 cups self-rising flour
3/4 tsp. apple pie spice

2 pears, peeled, cored, and
   diced
1/2 cup dried cranberries
for the frosting
14 oz. mascarpone

generous 1/2 cup confectioners'
   sugar, sifted
fresh cranberries and small
   holly leaves, to decorate

Preheat the oven to 350°F (180°C). Grease two 8-in. (20-cm.) round cake pans and line the bottoms with waxed paper.

Beat together the butter and sugar until pale and creamy, then beat in the eggs one at a time. Sift the flour and apple pie spice over the bowl, then fold in. Fold in the pears and cranberries.

Divide the mixture between the prepared pans, smoothing the top with the back of a spoon. Bake for 20 to 25 minutes until risen and golden and a skewer inserted in the center comes out clean. Transfer to a wire rack and let cool completely. To make the frosting, beat together the mascarpone and confectioners' sugar until smooth and creamy. Spread slightly less than half over one cake. Place the second cake on top and swirl the remaining frosting on top. Decorate with fresh cranberries and holly leaves.

Serves 8

simnel cake

see variations page 243

Simnel cake is the spiced, fruity cake topped with marzipan that is traditionally served in England at Easter. The classic Simnel Cake is covered with marzipan, while this one has a layer of marzipan running through the center.

for the cake
1 1/2 sticks butter, at room
    temperature
3/4 cup light brown sugar
3 eggs
scant 1 1/4 cups self-rising
    flour

1 oz. almonds, ground
2 tsp. apple pie spice
finely grated zest of 1 orange
finely grated zest of 1/2 lemon
1 3/4 cups mixed dried fruit
1/4 cup candied cherries
7 oz. marzipan, finely grated

to decorate
1 3/4 cups confectioners'
    sugar, sifted
2 tbsp. lemon juice
sugar-coated chocolate eggs,
    to decorate

Preheat oven to 325°F (160°C). Grease an 8-in. (20-cm.) round cake pan and line the base with waxed paper. Beat together the butter and brown sugar until smooth and creamy. Beat in the eggs one at a time, then sift the flour over the bowl. Add the ground almonds, apple pie spice, and orange and lemon zest, and fold together. Fold in the dried fruit and candied cherries. Spoon half the batter into the prepared pan, sprinkle with the grated marzipan, then spoon in the remaining batter. Smooth the top with the back of the spoon and bake for about 1 hour and 45 minutes, or until a skewer inserted in the center comes out clean. Let cool in the pan for about 10 minutes, then turn out onto a wire rack to cool completely. To decorate, stir together the confectioners' sugar and lemon juice until smooth, creamy, and pourable. Pour over the cake and decorate with the chocolate eggs.

Serves 8

christening cake

see variations page 244

This pretty lemon yellow cake is perfect for christenings and can be used for both boys and girls. The fresh zesty flavor will appeal to both children and adults, making it ideal for a family party.

for the cake
1 1/2 sticks butter, at room
   temperature
3/4 cup superfine sugar
finely grated zest of 1 lemon
3 eggs

scant 1 1/4 cups self-rising
   flour
to decorate
7 oz. mascarpone
7 oz. crème fraîche
3 tbsp. confectioners' sugar

finely grated zest of 1/2 lemon
yellow food coloring
white rice paper roses

Preheat the oven to 350°F (180°C). Grease two 8-in. (20-cm.) springform cake pans and line bottoms with waxed paper. Beat together the butter, sugar, and lemon zest until pale and fluffy. Beat in the eggs one at a time. Sift the flour over the mixture and stir in. Spoon the cake batter into the prepared pans and spread out evenly using the back of the spoon.

Bake for 20 to 25 minutes until golden brown and the cake springs back when pressed lightly with your fingertips. Turn the cakes out onto a wire rack, gently peel off the waxed paper, and let cool completely. To make the frosting, beat the mascarpone until soft, then beat in the crème fraîche, sugar, and lemon zest until smooth and creamy. Add a few drops of yellow food coloring to make a pale yellow. Spread slightly less than half the frosting over one of the cakes, then place the second cake on top. Swirl the remaining frosting on top and arrange white rice paper roses around the edge of the cake to decorate.

Serves 8

classic chocolate birthday cake

see variations page 245

A rich, melt-in-the-mouth chocolate cake studded with candles is the perfect choice for any birthday. Try this one swirled with a luscious chocolate buttercream.

for the cake
3 1/2 oz. semisweet chocolate
1 stick plus 1 tbsp. butter, at room temperature
3/4 cup superfine sugar
2 eggs, separated
scant 1 1/4 cups self-rising flour
1 tbsp. unsweetened cocoa powder
1/4 cup milk

for the frosting
3/4 stick butter, at room temperature
1 1/2 cups confectioners' sugar, sifted
1 tbsp. unsweetened cocoa powder
1 1/2 tbsp. milk
birthday candles, to decorate

Preheat the oven to 350°F (180°C). Grease an 8-in. (20-cm.) round springform pan and line the bottom with waxed paper.

Melt semisweet chocolate in a heatproof bowl set over a pan of barely simmering water, then set aside to cool for about 5 minutes. Beat together the butter and sugar, then beat in the egg yolks. Fold in the melted chocolate, then sift the flour and cocoa powder over the bowl. Stir in. Gradually stir in the milk to loosen the mixture.

In a clean bowl, whisk the egg whites until stiff, then fold them into the chocolate mixture, one-third at a time. Spoon the batter into the prepared cake pan and bake for about 45 minutes, or until a skewer inserted in the center comes out clean. Remove from the oven and turn out onto a wire rack to cool completely.

To make the frosting, beat the butter until soft and creamy, then sift the confectioners' sugar and cocoa powder over it. Add the milk. Beat until smooth and creamy. Swirl the frosting over the top of the cake. Decorate with birthday candles.

Serves 8

variations

white wedding cake

see base recipe page 211

small white wedding cake
Prepare the basic recipe, using two 5-in. (13-cm.) round cake pans. Fill each pan 3/4 inch deep with cake batter and discard the rest. Bake for about 20 minutes until golden and a skewer inserted in the center comes out clean.

large white wedding cake
Prepare the basic recipe, using two 11-in. (28-cm.) round cake pans and a double quantity of cake batter and frosting. Fill each pan 3/4 inch deep with cake batter and discard the rest. Bake until golden and a skewer inserted in the center comes out clean.

vanilla wedding cake
Prepare the basic recipe, replacing the lemon zest with 1 teaspoon vanilla extract.

floral wedding cake
Prepare the basic recipe, substituting 1 tablespoon rose water for the lemon zest and using pale pink rose petals to decorate the top.

variations

chocolate wedding cake

see base recipe page 212

small chocolate wedding cake
Prepare the basic recipe, using a 5-in. (13-cm.) springform cake pan. Fill the pan to about 1 inch deep with cake batter and discard the rest. Bake for about 35 minutes until firm.

large chocolate wedding cake
Prepare the basic recipe, using an 11-in. (28-cm.) round cake pan and a double quantity of cake batter and frosting. Fill the pan to about 1 inch deep with cake batter and discard the rest. Bake until firm to the touch and a skewer inserted in the center comes out clean.

chocolate passion wedding cake
Prepare the basic recipe, decorating the cake with dark red rose petals instead of the chocolate curls

summer berry chocolate wedding cake
Prepare the basic recipe, decorating the cake with fresh berries such as strawberries, raspberries, blueberries, and blackberries instead of chocolate curls.

variations

spring flower cake

see base recipe page 215

blueberry celebration cake
Prepare the basic recipe, omitting the sugared flowers. Instead, top the frosted cake with 1 2/3 cups fresh blueberries.

lemon & raspberry love cake
Prepare the basic recipe, adding a few drops of pink food coloring to the cream cheese frosting. Omit the sugared flowers and decorate the frosted cake with 2/3 cup fresh raspberries.

vanilla & strawberry birthday cake
Prepare the basic recipe, replacing the lemon zest with 1 teaspoon vanilla extract. Sprinkle about 2/3 cup quartered strawberries over the filling before topping with the second cake and frosting. Omit the sugared flowers and sprinkle with silver dragées and add birthday candles.

orange spring flower cake
Prepare the basic recipe, substituting finely grated orange zest for the lemon zest in the cake as well as the frosting. Substitute orange curd for the lemon curd in the filling.

variations

halloween cake

see base recipe page 216

nutty halloween cake
Prepare the basic recipe, adding 1/2 cup chopped walnuts with the mashed squash.

chocolate chip halloween cake
Prepare the basic recipe, adding 1/2 cup bittersweet chocolate chips with the mashed squash.

fruity halloween cake
Prepare the basic recipe, adding a generous 1/2 cup golden raisins with the mashed squash.

spicy halloween cake
Prepare the basic recipe, adding 1/2 teaspoon crushed dried chile flakes with the ginger and cinnamon. (The combination has a wonderful bite!)

citrus-spiced halloween cake
Prepare the basic recipe, adding the finely grated zest of 1 orange with the ginger and cinnamon.

variations

sparkling fireworks cake

see base recipe page 219

chocolate-orange fireworks cake
Prepare the basic recipe, replacing the vanilla with the finely grated zest of 1 orange.

mocha fireworks cake
Prepare the basic recipe, replacing the vanilla with 1 tablespoon instant coffee dissolved in 1 tablespoon boiling water.

chocolate chip fireworks cake
Prepare the basic recipe, sprinkling the cake with white chocolate chips instead of the silver dragées.

simple sparkling fireworks cake
Prepare the basic recipe, omitting the frosting. Instead, simply dust the cooled cake with cocoa powder, omit the silver dragées, and stud with sparklers.

loveheart valentine's cake

see base recipe page 220

raspberry valentine's cake
Prepare the basic recipe, substituting raspberries for the red currants
and raspberry jelly for the red currant jelly. Decorate the top with fresh
raspberries instead of the glitter, red currants, and white roses.

strawberry & red currant valentine's cake
Prepare the basic recipe, sandwiching the cake with strawberry jelly instead
of red currant jelly. Decorate the top with sliced strawberries instead of the
glitter, red currants, and white roses.

lemon valentine's cake
Prepare the basic recipe, substituting the finely grated zest of 1 lemon for
the vanilla. Omit the pink food coloring from the frosting and decorate with
red currants and pink rice paper roses.

red currant & passion fruit valentine's cake
Prepare the basic recipe. Omit the pink food coloring from the frosting.
Instead of the glitter, red currants, and roses, simply spoon the flesh of about
6 passion fruit over the frosting.

variations

ginger & lime ice cream birthday cake

see base recipe page 223

vanilla ice cream birthday cake
Omit the ginger and lime, and substitute Madeira Cake (page 64) for the ginger cake.

chocolate ice cream birthday cake
Fold 7 oz. melted bittersweet chocolate into the custard and omit the ginger and lime. Use Madeira Cake (page 64) instead of ginger cake.

coffee ice cream birthday cake
Stir 3 tablespoons instant coffee dissolved in 3 tablespoons boiling water into the custard and omit the ginger and lime. Use chocolate loaf cake instead of ginger cake.

strawberry ice cream birthday cake
Use only about half the custard. Omit the ginger and lime. Purée 4 cups fresh strawberries and strain purée into the custard. Decorate with fresh strawberries.

raspberry ice cream birthday cake
Use only about half the custard. Omit the ginger and lime. Purée 4 cups fresh raspberries and strain purée into the custard. Decorate with raspberries.

golden christmas cake

see base recipe page 224

silver christmas cake
Prepare the basic recipe, using edible silver powder, silver candy-coated almonds, and silver dragées instead of the gold decorations.

traditional christmas cake
Prepare the basic recipe, omitting the fondant shapes, candy almonds, and gold balls. Instead decorate the frosted cake with traditional decorations such as holly or snowmen.

snow white christmas cake
Prepare the basic recipe, omitting the gold powder and gold balls, and using only white candy-coated almonds.

variations

pear & cranberry christmas cake

see base recipe page 227

apple & cranberry Christmas cake
Prepare the basic recipe, substituting 1 large apple for the pears.

cinnamon, pear & cranberry christmas cake
Prepare the basic recipe, using 3/4 teaspoon ground cinnamon instead of the apple pie spice.

ginger, pear & cranberry christmas cake
Prepare the basic recipe, adding 3 chopped pieces of stem ginger in syrup with the pear and cranberries.

pear & cherry christmas cake
Prepare the basic recipe, substituting a scant 1/2 cup dried cherries for the cranberries.

variations

simnel cake

see base recipe page 228

chocolate simnel cake
Prepare the basic recipe, adding 3 tbsp. unsweetened cocoa powder to the flour.

flower-topped simnel cake
Prepare the basic recipe, omitting the sugar-coated eggs. Instead decorate with sugared flower petals (page 27).

traditional simnel cake
Prepare the basic recipe, omitting the decorations. Instead, brush the cooled cake with 1 tablespoon strained apricot jelly. Cover the cake with about 5 ounces of rolled out marzipan, and decorate the edge of the cake with bite-size balls of marzipan. Brush with egg white and bake at 425°F (220°C) for about 3 minutes until lightly browned.

ginger simnel cake
Prepare the basic recipe, adding 4 chopped pieces of stem ginger with syrup with the dried fruit.

cinnamon simnel cake
Prepare the basic recipe, substituting ground cinnamon for the apple pie spice.

variations

christening cake

see base recipe page 231

it's a boy! cake
Prepare the basic recipe, using pale blue food coloring instead of yellow in the frosting.

it's a girl! cake
Prepare the basic recipe, using pink food coloring instead of yellow, and pink rice paper flowers.

raspberry & lemon christening cake
Prepare the basic recipe, spreading the bottom layer with 3 tablespoons raspberry jelly before filling and decorating.

little boy blue christening cake
Prepare the basic recipe, omitting the yellow food coloring. Sprinkle about 1 2/3 cups blueberries over the filling before topping with the second cake, then decorate with more blueberries on top.

pretty-in-pink christening cake
Prepare the basic recipe, omitting the yellow food coloring. Arrange about 1 cup sliced strawberries on top of the filling before topping with the second cake, then decorate with more fresh strawberries on top.

variations

classic chocolate birthday cake

see base recipe page 232

chocolate-orange birthday cake
Prepare the basic recipe, adding the finely grated zest of 1 orange with
the egg yolks.

chocolate sandwich birthday cake
Prepare the basic recipe. When the cake has cooled, carefully cut it in
half horizontally with a serrated knife. Sandwich the cake with 3 to 4
tablespoons cherry jelly, then decorate as before.

mocha birthday cake
Prepare the basic recipe, adding 1 tablespoon instant coffee dissolved in
1 tablespoon boiling water with the milk.

dark & white chocolate birthday cake
Prepare the basic recipe, sprinkling the top of the frosted cake with white
chocolate chips before studding with candles.

cakes for special diets

The key ingredients in most cakes—butter, sugar, eggs, and flour—are frequently troublemakers for anyone following a special diet. But the good news is, whatever your dietary restrictions, there's a fabulous cake in this chapter just for you.

orange & almond cake

see variations page 269

Fresh and light, with a tender almond texture, this is the perfect cake for anyone avoiding wheat or gluten. Serve it for tea or dessert — it's good either way.

3 small oranges, peeled
6 eggs
1 cup superfine sugar
2 1/3 cups ground almonds

1 1/2 tsp. baking powder
confectioners' sugar, to dust
crème fraîche, to serve

Put the oranges in a saucepan and cover with boiling water. Simmer for 1 hour, then drain and let cool. Cut the cooled oranges in half and remove any seeds. Put the halved oranges in a food processor and blend to a smooth purée.

Meanwhile, preheat the oven to 350°F (180°C) and grease an 8-in. (20-cm.) round springform cake pan and line the bottom with waxed paper.

Pour the orange purée into a large bowl, then beat in the eggs. Stir in the sugar, then add the almonds and baking powder. Stir until well combined. Tip the mixture into the prepared cake pan and bake for about 1 hour until a skewer inserted in the center comes out clean. Let the cake cool in the pan before carefully unmolding.

Dust with confectioners' sugar and serve with crème fraîche.

Serves 8

moroccan-style yogurt cake

see variations page 270

This light and fluffy gluten-free cake is not unlike a cheesecake in taste and texture. Inspired by a classic Moroccan sweet, it is delicious served for dessert, drizzled with clear honey.

1/4 cup sour cream
9 oz. (1 cup) Greek yogurt
1 1/2 tbsp. cornstarch, dissolved in 1 1/2 tbsp. cold water
finely grated zest and juice of 1 lemon

finely grated zest of 1 orange
3 extra-large eggs, separated
1/3 cup superfine sugar
1/4 cup toasted almonds, chopped

Preheat the oven to 350°F (180°C). Grease an 8 x 10-in. (20 x 26-cm.) baking dish and line it with waxed paper.

Stir together the sour cream, yogurt, and cornstarch mixture until well mixed. Fold in the lemon zest and juice and the orange zest. In a separate bowl, whisk together the egg yolks and 1/4 cup of the sugar until thick and pale, then stir into the yogurt mixture. In another bowl, whisk the egg whites until they form peaks, then whisk in the remaining sugar. Fold the whites into the yogurt mixture, and pour into the lined baking dish.

Place the dish in a roasting pan. Pour in cold water to reach about halfway up the sides of the baking dish, then bake for 35 to 40 minutes. Remove the dish from the oven, sprinkle with the toasted almonds, and let cool. Serve at room temperature or chilled.

Serves 8

strawberry meringue layer cake

see variations page 271

Meringue is the ideal dessert for anyone on a gluten-free diet, and this simple cake sandwiched with strawberries and cream makes the perfect choice.

for the cake
scant 1 cup toasted hazelnuts
scant 1 1/2 cups superfine sugar
5 egg whites
2 tsp. white wine vinegar

for the filling
1/2 cup whipping cream
generous 1 cup fresh strawberries, hulled and
sliced, plus extra to serve

Preheat oven to 375°F (190°C). Grease two 8-in. (20-cm.) round springform cake pans and line the bottoms with waxed paper.

Put the nuts in a food processor and process until finely ground. Add about one-quarter of the sugar and stir together, then set aside. Whisk the egg whites until they form peaks, then gradually whisk in the remaining sugar until glossy and stiff. Sprinkle with the ground nuts and the vinegar, then fold in. Divide the mixture between the prepared pans and bake for about 40 minutes until pale and crisp. Turn off the oven and leave the meringues inside to cool completely.

To serve, peel the paper off the cooled meringues and place one "cake" upside down on a serving plate, so it has a flat top. Whip the cream and spread it over the top of the "cake." Top with sliced strawberries, then cover with the second "cake." Serve with more fresh strawberries on the side.

Serves 8

zucchini cake with lime & pistachio syrup

see variations page 272

Tender and sweet with the sharp zest of lime, this cake is the ideal choice for anyone on a dairy-free diet — and even those who aren't!

for the cake
2 extra-large eggs
generous 1/3 cup vegetable oil
1/2 cup superfine sugar
seeds from 6 cardamom pods,
    crushed
1/2 tsp. ground ginger

1 large (about 1/2 lb.) zucchini,
    grated
1/2 cup shelled pistachio nuts,
    chopped
1 1/3 cups self-rising flour
1/2 tsp. baking powder

for the syrup
finely grated zest and juice of
    2 limes
1/3 cup superfine sugar
1/2 cup shelled pistachio nuts,
    chopped

Preheat the oven to 350°F (180°C). Grease an 8-in. (20-cm.) round cake pan and line the bottom with waxed paper.

Beat together the eggs, oil, sugar, crushed cardamom, and ginger. Fold in the grated zucchini and chopped nuts. Sift the flour and baking powder over the bowl, then fold in. Spoon the mixture into the prepared pan, smoothing the top with the back of the spoon. Bake for about 35 minutes until risen and a skewer inserted in the center comes out clean. Let the cake cool in the pan for 5 minutes, then turn out onto a wire rack to cool completely.

To make the syrup, put the grated lime zest and lime juice in a pan and add the sugar. Warm gently, stirring, until the sugar has dissolved, then boil for 1 minute. Remove from the heat,

stir in the nuts, and let cool for 10 to 15 minutes to thicken. Pour the syrup over the cake and let it stand for at least 30 minutes before serving.

Serves 8

crispy cake

see variations page 273

This simple refrigerator cake is great for anyone avoiding gluten or eggs, but it's also a smashing cake for a kids' party. They just love crispy cakes! (For a less rich child-friendly version, press the mixture into just one pan and omit the mascarpone filling.)

9 oz. milk chocolate
1/4 stick butter
3 1/4 cups cornflakes
3/4 cup Brazil nuts, roughly chopped

2 1/2 oz. mini-marshmallows (or larger
    marshmallows snipped into pieces)
3 1/2 oz. mascarpone

Line the bottoms of two 8-in. (20-cm.) round springform pans with waxed paper. Break the chocolate into pieces and put them in a heatproof bowl with the butter. Place the bowl over a pan of barely simmering water and let the chocolate and butter melt. Remove from the heat, stir to combine, then let cool slightly.

Meanwhile, put the cornflakes in a bag and crush lightly with a rolling pin. Combine with the nuts and marshmallows, then stir into the melted chocolate. Divide the mixture between the two springform pans, spreading out in an even layer, then chill for about 1 1/2 hours until set.

To serve, carefully remove the two cakes from the pans, spread one with mascarpone, and place the second cake on top. Serve in small wedges.

Serves 8

dairy- & gluten-free sponge cake

see variations page 274

For anyone on a gluten- or dairy-free diet, this delicious cake layered with a thick soy custard and fresh strawberries is the perfect alternative to a traditional sponge cake.

for the cake
4 eggs, separated
2/3 cup superfine sugar
2 tbsp. cornstarch
2 tbsp. arrowroot
1/2 tsp. cream of tartar
1/2 tsp. baking soda

1 tbsp. light corn syrup, warmed
1 tsp. vanilla extract
for the filling
3 extra-large egg yolks
2 tbsp. superfine sugar
1 tbsp. all-purpose flour

1 cup soy milk
1 tsp. vanilla
to decorate
1 1/3 cups strawberries, quartered or sliced if large
confectioners' sugar, for dusting

Preheat oven to 350°F (180°C). Grease two 8-in. (20-cm.) round cake pans and line the bottom with waxed paper.

Put the egg whites in a clean, grease-free bowl and whisk to stiff peaks. Put the egg yolks, sugar, cornstarch, arrowroot, cream of tartar, baking soda, corn syrup, and vanilla in a separate bowl. Beat well. Fold yolk mixture into the egg whites. Pour into the prepared pans and bake for about 30 minutes until firm to the touch. Transfer cakes to a wire rack to cool completely.

Meanwhile, make the filling. Put the egg yolks, sugar, and flour in a bowl and whisk together until creamy. Heat the soy milk in a saucepan until almost boiling. Add the vanilla, then whisk into the egg mixture. Return to the pan and heat gently, stirring, until thick.

Pour into a bowl, press plastic wrap over the surface, cool, then chill. To serve, carefully slice the cake in half horizontally with a serrated knife. Spread the bottom layer with the soy custard, top with the strawberries, and then cover with the second cake. Dust with confectioners' sugar and serve.

Serves 8–10

pear & ginger cake

see variations page 275

Great for anyone on a dairy-free diet, this dense, moist cake with its delicate taste of pear and sugary, peppery bite of stem ginger makes a great choice for afternoon tea. Serve it plain or enjoy with heavy soy cream poured over the top.

3 eggs
2/3 cup vegetable oil
2 pears, grated
4 pieces of stem ginger in syrup, chopped
1 1/2 cups self-rising flour

1 tsp. baking powder
1 tsp. ground ginger
1/2 tsp. freshly grated nutmeg
generous 3/4 cup superfine sugar
confectioners' sugar, for dusting

Preheat the oven to 350°F (180°C). Grease an 8-in. (20-cm.) round cake pan and line the bottom with waxed paper.

Put the eggs and oil in a bowl and beat together to combine, then stir in the grated pears and stem ginger. Combine the flour, baking powder, ginger, nutmeg, and sugar, and sift over the egg mixture. Fold together until well mixed.

Pour the batter into the prepared pan and bake for about 1 hour until risen and golden and a skewer inserted in the center comes out clean. Let cake cool in the pan for a few minutes, then transfer to a wire rack to cool completely. Dust with confectioners' sugar to serve.

Serves 8

chocolate fudge cake

see variations page 276

Just because you're avoiding eggs and dairy, it doesn't mean you need to miss out. This incredibly quick and simple cake has a dark, moist texture and a rich, fudgy frosting.

for the cake
1 cup all-purpose flour
3/4 tsp. baking soda
4 tbsp. unsweetened cocoa
    powder

2/3 cup granulated sugar
2/3 cup water
4 tbsp. vegetable oil
1 tbsp. white wine vinegar

for the frosting
2 tbsp. vegetable oil
2 tbsp. unsweetened cocoa
2 tbsp. boiling water
1 cup confectioners' sugar,
    sifted

Preheat the oven to 350°F (180°C). Grease an 8-in. (20-cm.) round cake pan and line the bottom with waxed paper.

Sift the flour, baking soda, and cocoa into a bowl, then stir in the sugar and make a well in the middle. Pour the oil, vinegar, and water into the well and stir together quickly. Immediately pour the batter into the prepared pan and bake for about 25 minutes until risen and a skewer inserted in the center comes out clean. Turn out onto a wire rack and let cool completely.

To make the frosting, put the oil, cocoa, and boiling water in a heatproof bowl set over a pan of simmering water. Stir to combine, then gradually stir in the sugar and mix for about 2 minutes until thick and glossy. Add a drop or more water if too thick. Pour the frosting over the cake and let it set for a few minutes before serving.

Serves 8

low-fat orange cheesecake

see variations page 277

This chilled orange cheesecake is significantly lower in fat than many classic cheesecakes. Instead of rich and indulgent cream cheese, this recipe uses cottage cheese and fromage frais to produce a deliciously creamy cake with a distinctive texture.

1 1/4 cups finely ground graham cracker crumbs
1 3/4 oz. low-fat "margarine" spread, melted
10 oz. cottage cheese
7 oz. fat-free fromage frais (or substitute
   fromage blanc)

2/3 cup superfine sugar
finely grated zest of 2 large oranges
juice of 1 lemon
2 tsp. cornstarch, dissolved in 2 tsp. water
4 eggs

Grease an 8-in. (20-cm.) round springform cake pan. Stir crumbs into the melted low-fat spread. Press crumbs into the base of the prepared pan. Cover and chill for at least 30 minutes. Wrap the pan in two layers of aluminum foil.

Press the cottage cheese through a fine sieve twice, then beat with the fromage frais and sugar until smooth and creamy. Stir in the orange zest, lemon juice, and cornstarch mixture. Beat in the eggs one at a time.

Pour the mixture over the crumb base. Place the cake pan in a large roasting pan, then pour boiling water around the cake pan to about 1 to 1 1/2 inches deep. Bake for about 50 minutes until set (but still with a wobble in the center). Remove from the oven and let cool completely. Transfer to the refrigerator and chill for at least 4 hours before unmolding.

Serves 8

low-fat prune cake

see variations page 278

Simple and light, with a delightfully chewy texture and a subtle tang of prunes, this cake contains about half the fat of a regular frosted cake.

for the cake
2 3/4 oz. dried prunes
3 tbsp. boiling water
1 stick butter, at room
    temperature

2/3 cup superfine sugar
3 eggs
scant 1 1/4 cups self-rising
    flour

to decorate
1 1/3 cups confectioners'
    sugar, sifted
2 tbsp. lemon juice
12 dried prunes

Put the prunes in a bowl, cover with the boiling water, and let soak for 2 hours. Blend to a smooth purée in a food processor or blender.

Preheat the oven to 350°F (180°C). Grease an 8-in. (20-cm.) springform round or square cake pan and line the bottom with waxed paper.

Beat the butter until creamy, then beat in the prune purée, followed by the sugar. Beat until smooth. Beat in the eggs one at a time, then sift the flour over the bowl and fold in.

Spoon the batter into the cake pan and spread out evenly. Bake for about 30 minutes until risen and golden and a skewer inserted in the center comes out clean. Let cool in the pan for about 5 minutes, then turn out onto a wire rack to cool completely. To decorate, stir together the confectioners' sugar and lemon juice until smooth and creamy. Pour over the cake. Decorate with the prunes and serve cut into squares.

Serves 8

low-fat lemon berry cake

see variations page 279

Simple and summery, this fresh and fruity layer cake is just the thing if you're watching your weight. The cake is best eaten on the day it's made.

for the cake
3 eggs
1/3 cup superfine sugar
1/3 cup self-rising flour, sifted
finely grated zest of 1 lemon
3 tbsp. melted butter

to decorate
9 oz. fat-free fromage frais or fromage blanc
3 1/2 to 4 tbsp. lemon curd
about 1 1/2 cups fresh berries, such as blueberries, strawberries, raspberries, and red currants

Preheat the oven to 350°F (180°C). Grease two 8-in. (20-cm.) round cake pans and line the bottoms with waxed paper.

Put the eggs and sugar in a bowl over a pan of barely simmering water, making sure the bowl does not touch the water. Whisk for about 10 minutes until the mixture is thick and pale and leaves a trail when the whisk is lifted out of the bowl. Sift about three-quarters of the flour over the mixture and fold in. Sift in the remaining flour, sprinkle in the lemon rind, and gradually drizzle in the butter as you fold together. Spoon the batter into the prepared pans and bake for about 30 minutes until risen and golden and a skewer inserted in the center comes out clean. Turn out on a wire rack to cool completely. Just before serving, stir together the fromage frais and lemon curd, checking the flavor and adding a little more lemon curd if needed. Spread slightly less than half over one of the cakes and top with the second cake. Swirl the remaining fromage frais over the top and decorate with fresh berries.

Serves 8

low-fat beet & carrot cake

see variations page 280

Lower in fat than a classic frosted carrot cake, this rich, sweet, dense cake is flecked with ruby red shreds of beet. Even if you don't like beets, you'll love this cake.

for the cake
1 1/2 cups self-rising flour
1 1/2 tsp. baking powder
2/3 cup light brown sugar
1 tsp. ground cinnamon
1/2 tsp. ground ginger
1 large banana, mashed

1 medium carrot, grated
1 beet, grated (about 1 1/2
    inches in diameter)
2 eggs, beaten
2/3 cup vegetable oil

for the frosting
3 1/2 oz. fat-free or low-fat
    fromage frais or fromage
    blanc
2 tbsp. confectioners' sugar,
    sifted
1 tsp. finely grated lemon zest

Preheat the oven to 350°F (180°C). Grease an 8-in. (20-cm.) round cake pan and line the bottom with waxed paper.

Combine the flour, baking powder, brown sugar, and spices in a large bowl. Make a well in the center. Add the banana, carrot, beet, eggs, and oil. Stir to combine thoroughly.

Tip the batter into the prepared pan, level the surface, and bake for about 45 minutes until risen and golden and a skewer inserted in the center comes out clean. Turn out onto a wire rack and let cool completely.

To make the frosting, stir together the fromage frais, sugar, and lemon zest. Swirl frosting on top of the cake.

Serves 8

orange & almond cake

see base recipe page 247

orange, cinnamon & almond cake
Prepare the basic recipe, adding 1 teaspoon ground cinnamon.

orange, cardamom & almond cake
Prepare the basic recipe, adding the crushed seeds of 6 cardamom pods.

orange & lemon cake
Prepare the basic recipe, adding the finely grated zest of 1 lemon.

orange, chile & almond cake
Prepare the basic recipe, adding 1/4 teaspoon crushed dried chile flakes.

orange, ginger & almond cake
Prepare the basic recipe, adding 1 teaspoon ground ginger. Stir in 2 chopped pieces of stem ginger in syrup with the almonds.

moroccan-style yogurt cake

see base recipe page 248

vanilla yogurt cake
Prepare the basic recipe, substituting 1 1/2 teaspoons vanilla extract for the grated orange zest.

pistachio yogurt cake
Prepare the basic recipe, substituting roughly chopped pistachios for the almonds.

hazelnut yogurt cake
Prepare the basic recipe, substituting roughly chopped toasted hazelnuts for the almonds.

cinnamon yogurt cake
Prepare the basic recipe, stirring 1 teaspoon ground cinnamon into the yogurt mixture and omitting the orange zest.

blueberry yogurt cake
Prepare the basic recipe, sprinkling about 1 1/3 cups fresh blueberries over the top of the chilled cake.

strawberry meringue layer cake

see base recipe page 251

raspberry meringue layer cake
Prepare the basic recipe, using whole fresh raspberries instead of the strawberries.

blueberry meringue layer cake
Prepare the basic recipe, using whole fresh blueberries instead of the strawberries.

lemon meringue layer cake
Prepare the basic recipe, folding 4 tablespoons lemon curd into the whipped cream before spreading it over the cake.

summer berry meringue layer cake
Prepare the basic recipe, replacing the strawberries with a mixture of fresh berries.

grape meringue layer cake
Prepare the basic recipe, using halved seedless grapes instead of the strawberries.

zucchini cake with lime & pistachio syrup

see base recipe page 252

zucchini cake with cream cheese frosting
Prepare the basic recipe, omitting the lime syrup. Instead frost with the cream cheese frosting from the classic carrot cake (page 63). Use soy "cream cheese" for a dairy-free cake.

zucchini & walnut cake
Prepare the basic recipe, substituting walnuts for the pistachios.

spiced zucchini cake
Prepare the basic recipe, substituting 1/2 teaspoon apple pie spice for the cardamom seeds.

fiery zucchini cake
Prepare the basic recipe, adding 1/4 teaspoon crushed dried chile flakes with the cardamom seeds.

zucchini & pecan cake
Prepare the basic recipe, substituting pecans for the pistachios.

variations

crispy cake

see base recipe page 255

chocolate & hazelnut crispy cake
Prepare the basic recipe, using roughly chopped toasted hazelnuts instead of Brazil nuts.

chocolate & almond crispy cake
Prepare the basic recipe, substituting roughly chopped toasted almonds for the Brazil nuts.

white chocolate crispy cake
Prepare the basic recipe, using white chocolate instead of milk chocolate.

colored sprinkle crispy cake
Prepare the basic recipe. After spreading the mixture in the pans, shake multicolored sprinkles over one of the cakes. Use this as the top cake when you assemble the chilled cakes with the filling.

white chocolate crunch
Prepare the basic recipe. Drizzle the finished cake with about 1/4 cup melted white chocolate.

variations

dairy- & gluten-free sponge cake

see base recipe page 256

dairy- & gluten-free victoria sandwich
Prepare the basic recipe, omitting the filling. Simply sandwich the cake with 3 to 4 tablespoons of your favorite jelly, then dust with confectioners' sugar.

blueberry dairy- & gluten-free sponge
Prepare the basic recipe, substituting blueberries for the strawberries.

raspberry dairy- & gluten-free sponge
Prepare the basic recipe, substituting raspberries for the strawberries.

lemon dairy- & gluten-free sponge
Prepare the basic recipe, substituting the finely grated zest of 1 lemon for the vanilla in the cake.

cherry dairy- & gluten-free sponge
Prepare the basic recipe, substituting cherries for the strawberries.

pear & ginger cake

see base recipe page 259

frosted pear & ginger cake
Prepare the basic recipe, but do not dust the cooled cake with confectioners' sugar. Instead, beat together 2 cups sifted confectioners' sugar, 1 stick plus 2 tablespoons soft butter, 2 teaspoons lemon juice, and 2 tablespoons ginger syrup (from the jar of stem ginger) until smooth and creamy. Swirl over the cake.

pear, golden raisin & ginger cake
Prepare the basic recipe, adding 2/3 cup golden raisins to the batter.

pear, cherry & ginger cake
Prepare the basic recipe, adding 1/2 cup dried cherries to the batter.

pear, hazelnut & ginger cake
Prepare the basic recipe, adding 1/2 cup chopped toasted hazelnuts to the batter.

pear, almond & ginger cake
Prepare the basic recipe, adding 1/2 cup chopped toasted almonds to the batter.

variations

chocolate fudge cake

see base recipe page 260

chocolate & orange fudge cake
Prepare the basic cake recipe, using orange juice instead of the water, and adding the finely grated zest of 1 orange with the oil and vinegar.

mocha fudge cake
Prepare the basic cake recipe, adding 1 tablespoon instant coffee dissolved in 1 tablespoon boiling water with the oil and vinegar. For the frosting, dissolve 1 tablespoon instant coffee in the boiling water before mixing with the sugar.

chocolate cinnamon cake
Prepare the basic recipe, adding 1 teaspoon ground cinnamon with the flour.

chocolate rum cake
Prepare the basic recipe, adding 1 tablespoon rum with the oil and vinegar.

chocolate raspberry cake
Prepare the basic recipe, topping the frosted cake with fresh raspberries.

variations

low-fat orange cheesecake

see base recipe page 263

low-fat lemon cheesecake
Prepare the basic recipe, substituting the finely grated zest of 1 lemon for the orange zest.

full-fat orange cheesecake
Who cares about calories! Use full-fat cream cheese instead of the cottage cheese, and sour cream instead of the fat-free fromage frais. (Don't worry about straining the cream cheese; just go ahead and beat it with the sour cream and sugar.)

ricotta orange cheesecake
Prepare the basic recipe, substituting ricotta for the cottage cheese. The ricotta needn't be strained.

low-fat ginger & orange cheesecake
Prepare the basic recipe, using gingersnap crumbs instead of graham cracker crumbs.

low-fat orange & vanilla cheesecake
Prepare the basic recipe, adding 1 1/2 teaspoons vanilla extract with the grated orange zest and juice.

variations

low-fat prune cake

see base recipe page 264

not-so-low-fat chocolate & prune cake
Prepare the basic recipe, omitting the frosting. Instead, chop 3 1/2 ounces bittersweet chocolate and put the pieces in a bowl. Heat a scant 1/2 cup of whipping cream until almost boiling, then pour it over the chocolate and let stand for about 5 minutes. Stir until smooth, then set aside until thickened. Pour over the cake. Decorate with more prunes on top if you like.

low-fat cinnamon prune cake
Add 3/4 teaspoon ground cinnamon to the batter.

low-fat ginger prune cake
Prepare the basic recipe, adding 1/2 teaspoon ground ginger to the batter, then fold in 3 chopped pieces of stem ginger in syrup.

low-fat prune & orange cake
Prepare the basic recipe, adding the finely grated zest of 1 orange to the prune purée.

low-fat prune & armagnac cake
Prepare the basic recipe using 1 1/2 tablespoons Armagnac and 1 1/2 tablespoons boiling water to soak the prunes.

variations

low-fat lemon berry cake

see base recipe page 267

low-fat lemon cherry cake
Prepare the basic recipe, using fresh pitted cherries instead of the berries.

low-fat orange berry cake
Prepare the basic recipe, using the finely grated zest of 1 orange instead of the lemon zest and orange curd instead of the lemon curd.

low-fat lemon peach cake
Prepare the basic recipe, using pitted and peeled (fresh or canned) peaches instead of the berries.

low-fat lemon fig cake
Prepare the basic recipe, using wedges of fresh figs instead of the berries.

low-fat lemon mango cake
Prepare the basic recipe, using wedges of fresh mango instead of the berries.

variations

low-fat beet & carrot cake

see base recipe page 268

low-fat beet cake
Prepare the basic recipe, using 2 beets and omitting the carrot.

low-fat carrot cake
Prepare the basic recipe, using 2 carrots and omitting the beet.

low-fat carrot & apple cake
Prepare the basic recipe, using 1 small grated apple instead of the beet.

low-fat carrot & zucchini cake
Prepare the basic recipe, using 1/2 grated zucchini instead of the beet.

nutty carrot & beet cake
Prepare the basic recipe, adding 1/2 cup chopped walnuts with the grated carrot and beet.

index

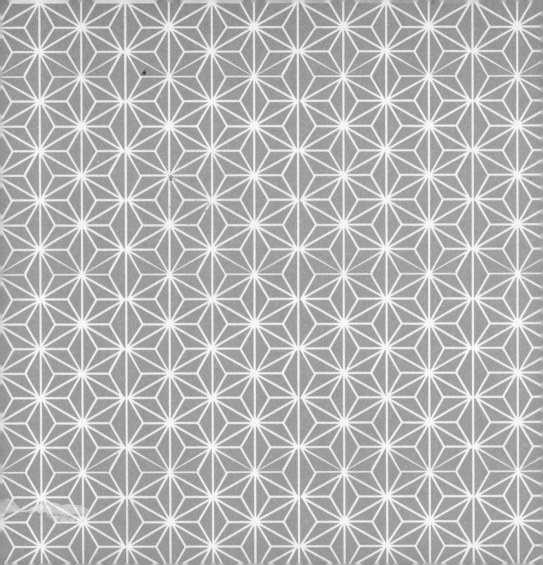